P9-CIU-055

UNPLUGGED PLAY

TODDLER

155 ACTIVITIES &
GAMES FOR AGES 1-2

BOBBI CONNER

WORKMAN PUBLISHING * NEW YORK

For Cassidy, Olivia, and Peter

Copyright © 2020 by Bobbi Conner
Illustrations copyright © 2020 by Bart Aalbers

This book has been adapted from *Unplugged Play*
(Workman Publishing, 2007).

Library of Congress Cataloging-in-Publication Data is available.

ISBN 978-1-5235-1018-4

Design by Rae Ann Spitzenberger
Paper texture photo by sompunya/Shutterstock.com

Workman books are available at special discounts when purchased in bulk for premiums and sales promotions as well as for fund-raising or educational use. Special editions or book excerpts can also be created to specification. For details, contact the Special Sales Director at the address below, or send an email to specialmarkets@workman.com.

Workman Publishing Co., Inc.
225 Varick Street
New York, NY 10014-4381
workman.com

WORKMAN is a registered trademark of Workman Publishing Co., Inc.

Printed in China
First printing July 2020

10 9 8 7 6 5 4 3 2 1

CONTENTS

PLAY MATTERS
WHY—AND HOW—I WROTE THIS BOOK

Children like to play. And why wouldn't they? It's fun! So it makes sense that the more they play, the more they will want to play again. It's a lovely, self-perpetuating cycle that most parents intuitively understand. But what is harder to grasp is the power of play to shape a child's world, particularly a world that is high-tech, fast paced, and plugged in.

And that's why I wrote this book. During my twenty years as host of the nationally syndicated *Parent's Journal* public radio show, I've chatted with many of the leaders in the world of child development. Whether it was David Elkind or Penelope Leach, Fred Rogers or Benjamin Spock, they all—every one of them—spoke of the significance of play. And now I want to help parents help their children enjoy the wholesome, old-fashioned experience of playing creatively and freely . . . *without technology*. I started by collecting and inventing hundreds of games, and then I tested them one by one on different groups of children, ages twelve months to ten years. When the kids rejected a game or an activity, I rejected it too. When a game inspired them to come up with a variation of their own, I appropriated their invention. The result is the more than one hundred "unplugged" games that you have here.

But why "unplugged," you may ask. Since most of us embrace technology to some extent every day—can you imagine a world without email?—it may seem far-fetched to suggest that parents minimize the amount of time their child spends connected to anything with a screen, a plug, or a battery. Besides, it's so easy to plunk a kid in front of a screen! But children need to interact with living, breathing human playmates, and not be held captive by the lights, sounds, and images on a screen. They need to run, chase, ride, skip, and jump, and not *sit still* for prolonged blocks of time. We need only look at the huge rise in childhood obesity to understand how children suffer physically when they remain inactive.

But the toll on kids who rely primarily on electronics for their entertainment goes way beyond some extra pounds. When a child sits in front of a screen, he has no opportunity to connect with the natural world—mud, water, sand, stones, leaves, seeds, animals, insects, sunshine, and rain. It might not seem like such a huge loss in the moment when your child is contentedly clicking buttons on the keypad, but there is something essential about a child getting his hands messy. In addition, because electronic games are preprogrammed with finite possible responses, they limit the imagination. A child who draws, paints, builds, and invents knows a creativity that has no boundaries. By learning that she has the ability to shape her world—either alone or in the company of others—she gains the self-confidence she needs to grow into a problem-solving, creative adult.

And who could ask for more?

—*Bobbi Conner*

THE

POWER

OF PLAY

ou may feel as though life has changed in an essential way, and that there is no time for the kind of old-fashioned, wholesome, playful childhood that you had envisioned for your child. But there are the same twenty-four hours in each day and the same seven days in each week. What's changed is the pace of life.

To a large extent, you, as the parent, are the keeper of the time in your family. You arrange the family schedule; you set dinnertime, bath time, and bedtime; and you get your child to appointments, childcare, playgroups, and school *on time*. As the keeper of the time, you have the power and authority to slow time down. And if you make that choice, you'll probably find that your child has more time for all sorts of unplugged play.

Let me give you an example from my own life as a mom. When my son was in kindergarten and my daughter was three, I worked full time. I was a single parent earning a living for our family of three by day and doing all the typical parenting tasks by night. I always felt rushed. I picked my children up from their Montessori school each day at 5:00 P.M. and headed home. The moment I walked in the door I jumped right into making dinner. (And in the back of my mind I was thinking about the time needed for baths, bedtime stories, and laundry too.) So I scurried around the kitchen while the children played on their own. Or at least that's what they were supposed to do. Often, after just a minute or two, a sibling squabble would set off a group meltdown.

This went on for several days in a row that first week of school, and I realized something needed to change. The next day I put a happier plan in place. I walked in the house and said to my children, "Let's get a snack and read a story together!" (I meant now, not later tonight.) We grabbed three apples from the fruit bowl and a small plate of sliced cheese. We went into the living room, snuggled up on the couch, and ate our snack while I began to read *Caps for Sale*. It was a nourishing, calming time, and after fifteen minutes my son said, "I want to play with my LEGOs now." My daughter said, "Me too." Off they went. I started dinner knowing everyone was happy and reconnected. We all had the time and attention we needed to make a graceful transition into our evening together as a family. Our new after-work and after-school routine made an immediate, positive difference in our lives over the years. I often recalled how I had *slowed down time* and applied this same smart thinking whenever our routine or mood felt off-kilter.

> "Play is not trivial. When children play, they're doing important work."
>
> **—Fred Rogers**
> Emmy Award–winning creator and host of *Mister Rogers' Neighborhood*

I mention this lesson from my own life for three reasons. One, to assure you that simple solutions are often best for fixing family routines that are out of sync. Two, to encourage you to stop, take a breath, and make whatever changes are necessary to diminish that anxious feeling that comes when time closes in on you. And finally, to remind you that *children need time to play*. It was true when *you* were a child, and it is just as true for children today.

DARE TO UNPLUG

Play is fun, which is the primary reason children want to do it. And the more fun children have while they play, the more they want to play again next time. This basic cause-and-effect law keeps children in perpetual motion, in search of more and more fun and more and more play. But the full story about play doesn't end here. Play is also a powerful way for children to experience the world.

Children learn through their everyday play experiences. In fact, play is perhaps the best way for children to learn about themselves (and their own capabilities), to learn about one another, and to learn how all things work in the world. What's absolutely brilliant about this evolutionary mechanism is that children don't know and don't particularly care about the learning component to their play. For example, when two little toddlers play side by side, each loading miniature blocks into their own dump truck, they don't see small hints of cooperation, sharing, or a budding friendship unfolding. They are just doing what toddlers love to do. Physical, intellectual, social, and emotional growth are happening as children go about the everyday business of play.

We parents can't be satisfied, however, with knowing that our children are out there playing, either alone or with others. We need to do everything in our power to encourage *unplugged* play—those marvelous, nonelectronic, time-tested games and activities that build strong bodies (climbing, hopping, running, jumping, tossing, catching), expand the mind (guessing, figuring, remembering, numbering, interpreting), spark creativity (inventing, building, wordplay, making jokes, telling stories, drawing, painting, singing songs), and forge friendships.

THE SIMPLE PLEASURES

Play is serious business when it comes to a child's health and development, according to the American Academy of Pediatrics (AAP). The AAP clinical report, *The Power of Play*, explains how and why playing with parents and peers is the key to building thriving brains, bodies, and social bonds. Here are some of the benefits of play:

- Helps prevent obesity, heart disease, and diabetes
- Builds strong bones and muscles
- Improves an overall sense of well-being
- Improves sleep
- Burns calories
- Diffuses stress
- Boosts self-esteem

Research also shows that play can improve children's ability to plan and organize, get along with others, regulate emotions, and strengthen language and math skills.

Here are just a few of the sensations and experiences that come alive through unplugged play. When you read this list, the essential question to ask yourself is: Can a screen or machine bring the same joyful experience into my child's life?

Play for Joy

- Run around with a friend.
- Squish your toes and fingers in mud.
- Feel the sunshine on your face as you swing higher and higher.
- Make your own music with shakers, rattles, and bells.
- Run through the sprinkler in the backyard.
- Zoom cars and trucks down a cardboard ramp.

- Chase after butterflies.
- Have a picnic with your teddy bear.

Play for Intelligence

- Discover which pans make the loudest noises when you hit them with a spoon.
- Point out animals, characters, and objects in a book.
- Memorize favorite songs and know when to clap or stomp your feet.
- Stack colored rings in order, with the biggest on the bottom and the littlest ones on top.

Play for Connection

- Listen to a story and know when it's time to turn the page.
- Play peekaboo again and again with someone you love.
- Make a birthday crown (with a parent) and wear it on your head.
- Use a roller, paint, and paper to make a giant outdoor painting.
- Put on a costume and pretend to be a grown-up.
- Play kitchen soccer and clap each time the ball rolls in the laundry basket.
- Turn a big cardboard box into a truck for all your stuffed animals.
- Spread finger paint on a cookie sheet and watch colorful shapes emerge.
- Chase bubbles around the lawn with playmates.
- Play Follow the Leader for the very first time.
- Dance to music with others.
- Create drawings alongside a friend.
- Build a fort under the kitchen table with a parent.

Children will learn to stretch their attention spans and manage their emotions. They will become the masters of their own destiny and directors of their own experience. This is true in the first year of life and every week, month, and year thereafter. Children will also learn that they are capable of entertaining and amusing themselves, without machines and without an adult!

Within this broad category of unplugged play, there are many types of games for your child to experience. First up are the loads of clever and creative games a child can play alone— on-the-spot activities that parents can offer whenever they need a few minutes to make dinner, work, or chat on the phone. But teaching kids how to amuse themselves is not some selfish act; rather, showing them that they don't have to reach for a screen whenever a parent or friend is not around is a lifelong gift.

And then, of course, there are hundreds upon hundreds of games to play with one or two friends, or with large

groups (such as at birthday parties or playgroups)—the absolute best way for a child to develop social skills, again, whatever the child's age. This holds true for the shy child, the child who gravitates toward one particular playmate, or the child who thrives in a large group. Play is a magnificent way to learn to get along with others, to take turns, to negotiate; it also teaches children about fairness, making amends, and what it feels like to have a friend.

Finally, there are games that parents and children can enjoy together, in the park or at the kitchen table. Bringing an entire family together creates another wonderful tradition of play (see Family Game Night, page 200). I've tried to include games that do not require an adult to wear a donkey hat or sing "Yankee Doodle Dandy" while standing on one foot. But far be it from me to tell you to put dignity in the way of a good time!

> If you've been around kids, particularly young kids, for any length of time, [you know] it's absolutely true that all the most important things in life are learned through play."
>
> **—Penelope Leach, PhD**
> psychologist and author
> of *Your Baby and Child*

WHAT'S WRONG WITH ELECTRONIC PLAY?

Okay, I can hear you muttering in the background—*what world does she live in?*—so it's time to get real. I am not suggesting that electronic games and high-tech play have no place in a child's world, but I feel very strongly that they should occupy only a minor amount of a child's playtime.

Do you want to know why? I've covered some of these points earlier, but they're worth reiterating. To begin with, many children play these games in isolation. So rather than interacting with human playmates, they're being captivated by lights, sounds, and moving images. The ramifications on developing social skills (and friendships) are huge. Furthermore, it's a good bet that your child will not be running around while playing on a screen. (Is it any wonder that we are witnessing a huge rise in childhood obesity?) And it's not just the physical benefits that he'll be missing. When your child draws, paints, builds, and invents, or sings songs, listens to poems and stories, there are no artificial boundaries or predetermined limits to his creativity. And when she's playing outside, there's even more—in the form of mud, water, sand, stones, leaves, seeds, animals, insects, sunshine, rain.

FIGHTING THE FIGHT: NOT GIVING IN TO HIGH-TECH PRESSURE

Given all this, you may be wondering how in the world these technology-based games have become so popular—they're *always* there, and nearly everyone seems to be playing them. The short answer has to do with successful advertising. The longer answer includes peer pressure, the mistaken belief among parents and educators that children must learn to be proficient on the computer at age four or five or ten or they will be left in the dust academically, and the fact that playing a video to amuse a child is just easier to do when you need a quiet moment for yourself.

But that's only part of the story. Put a toddler in front of a large screen with bright, quick-moving images, and chances are his eyes will light up and he will follow the movement on the screen with intensity. Now add interesting sounds, and your child's auditory attention will be fixed on that as well. So your child appears to be having fun. That's one thing. The other is that high-tech gadgets are so much a part of our adult lives—and we value them so highly—that we imagine they must be of use to children too. And they can be. Children with physical limitations or special needs can really benefit from gadgets and games that allow them to connect to friends. And all children, once they get into school, will need to learn to use computers and tablets and phones. But hold back. Children are not mini adults.

DIBS: A THREE-STEP ACTION PLAN

My best advice is to treat high-tech play like a hot fudge sundae—perfectly fine for now and then, but not for every day. Easy for me to say! And not so easy for you to do. But here's a three-point action plan called DIBS that may help.

1. Delay introducing your child to high-tech toys, computers, and electronic games during the infant, toddler, preschool, and kindergarten years, when your child's brain is growing rapidly and incorporating all the social, emotional, and physical development that comes with that. Educational psychologist Jane M. Healy, author of *Your Child's Growing Mind*, has studied children's use of computers for years and has concluded that they will *not* be disadvantaged if they are not introduced to computers until age seven or eight.

2. Introduce your child to the habit of having fun without plug-ins. That's what this book is for! Let the pleasure of good old-fashioned play win your child's heart.

3. Be selective and deliberate about how much time you allow for electronic play in your child's week and which games are okay. Make a specific Electronic Play Plan for your family and stick to it. (See suggestions from other families on the next page.)

EIGHT WAYS TO PROMOTE A NO-TECH ZONE

1 Provide toys that allow variety—balls, a sandbox, building blocks, art supplies, etc.

2 Change it up by encouraging all types of play: high-energy and physical play, quiet games, arts, crafts, music, building, and imaginative play. Relax. Unplugged play is fun. Children don't need to know that it's often educational. Look for small windows of opportunity that can flow seamlessly into your day—set your toddler up for a ten- or fifteen-minute game of Shake, Rattle-n-Roll, page 38, while you do chores, start a silly guessing game at the dinner table, tell a story in the car on the drive across town. Keep it casual. Keep it short.

3 Make your home a place that other children enjoy visiting. It's easier to control what kinds of games kids play on your own turf.

4 Don't hover, and don't micromanage your child's play. Let her explore matters on her own. Simply offer a quick demo about using a toy or a new material (if needed), and then back off.

5 If your child looks stumped, toss out a play-inducing challenge: "What sort of tower could you make with these blocks?"

6 Don't be afraid to let grandparents, friends, and gift givers know you prefer low-tech or no-tech toys for your child. And until your child is in school, try to keep him away from high-tech anything.

7 As kids get older, set up a Family Electronic Play Plan. You—not your child—should decide how much time is allowed for electronic play each week and when to fit it into your routine. Some families limit electronic toys and play to weekends. You'll know best what works for you. (See what the American Academy of Pediatrics recommends to curb electronic play, page 11.)

8 Create a regular time that is Family Game Night—once a month or once a week—and put it on your calendar so you don't forget. (See Family Game Night ideas, page 200.)

MAKE AN ELECTRONIC PLAY PLAN

Time for another reality check: The American Academy of Pediatrics (AAP) recommends that screen time (digital media) for children under two years of age should be very limited, and only when an adult is standing by to co-view, talk, and teach (for example, video-chatting with family). If you do want to introduce digital media to children eighteen to twenty-four months, the AAP recommends that you choose high-quality programming and avoid solo media use.

For children two to five years old, the AAP recommends that parents limit screen use to no more than one hour of high-quality programming per day. This includes time spent using digital games, computers, tablets, smartphones, and television.

As your child gets older, screen time becomes more difficult to control. That's why it's important to set these boundaries early on. Here are some specific plans that other families have used to limit electronic play and screen time during the toddler stage:

▸ Encourage small moments of independent play for your toddler each day with safe, toddler-friendly toys that are easy to manipulate and encourage open-ended, freestyle play. (When your child experiences a few happy moments of playing on her own each day, she gets comfortable and confident with the idea of being the master of her own play.)

▸ Enjoy freestyle family playtime on a regular basis. This approach makes unplugged play a normal (and expected) part of your toddler's routine.

▸ Connect with other families in your community who value and encourage unplugged, active playtime.

- Host occasional unplugged playgroups with other toddlers (and parents) and have an assortment of unplugged toys and playthings for all.

- When celebrating a holiday or birthday, include playtime and games in your get-togethers with family and friends. Just as you would plan ahead with the food, gather up a few favorite toys, props, and playthings ahead of time to encourage fun for all.

- Read aloud to your toddler on a daily basis and encourage your child to turn the page and point out characters, nature, and colors. Let your child linger on each page and see what catches his eye. Make reading aloud a playful and interactive experience!

- Make music, singing, and dancing playful and routine parts of your family's life.

All of these nonelectronic playtime ideas set expectations for your young child as he learns what it means to invent his own play and how to play happily with others.

MAKE YOURS AN UNPLUGGED COMMUNITY

Parents who set limits for their children with electronic toys sometimes feel as though they are swimming upstream. To tackle this problem, find other parents who are also swimming upstream and include them in your social circle. Plan potluck dinners with the parents and playdates with the children (or parent and child play parties). Also, organize informal Unplugged Play Parties for small groups of two to four children, with each family involved taking a turn hosting a playdate at their home once a month. There's no need to make these playdate parties especially elaborate or terribly structured. Just provide a little bit of kid-friendly food and opportunities to play indoors and outdoors.

HOW TO USE THIS BOOK

All of the games in this book are intended for toddlers age one to two. You'll find that the games are organized by situation. Who's playing? Just your child? Look in the "Solo Play" section. You and your child? Flip to "Parent & Child Play." For two to four children, check out the "Play with Others" pages, and lastly, for foolproof party plans, the "Party Play" games will have you covered.

There are games for rainy days and sunny days, games that last five minutes and games that can stretch on for longer blocks of time. Do you need a solo game to amuse your toddler while you cook dinner tonight? If so, a quick skim through the Busy-Body pages will give you lots of ideas for those moments when you have only a bit of time or when you need to keep your toddler occupied while you're busy with some activity nearby. (Try Hallway Bag-Ball on page 40; all you need is a paper bag and a few tennis balls.) For longer chunks of time, Spontaneous Play provides

TOYS FOR CHILDREN WITH SPECIAL NEEDS

Specialized toys are available for children with motor delays or impairment, visual or hearing impairment, language delays, and a range of other special needs. Beyond Play is a great online source to help you find toys and play suggestions tailored to your child's abilities. Their website, www.beyondplay.com, features more than 1,000 toys and products you can order directly, along with useful articles and play tips. The "search by product" feature also helps you find toys suited to your child's developmental stage.

plenty of ideas for ways to get your child moving, inventing, and creating on her own.

Enjoy the freedom to move through the pages of this book to discover games that will engage your child. And then encourage your child to tweak the games to suit her style, interests, and abilities.

If your child has a physical delay or disability, or cognitive, social, or speech delays or disabilities, you'll find tons of games in these pages that offer fabulous opportunities for your child to have fun and at the same time work on targeted goals, such as increasing muscle strength, cardiovascular endurance, or motor or speech development. Perhaps, for example, your child has trouble flexing his arms or reaching and grasping. There are loads of catching and tossing activities to help fine-tune those skills. Some of these games use balls of various sizes and others use beanbags, which may make tossing, catching, and grasping a bit easier for a child with motor delays or disabilities. (You can even substitute a silk neck scarf for a ball or beanbag to invent a new variation of catch that allows extra time for catching the floating scarf.) As in all cases, you know your child best. Select games (and invent variations) that allow just the right balance of challenge and success. When you discover a game that hits this mark, you'll know—your child will want to play again and again.

If your child has difficulty picking up on social cues, many of the Play with Others games are perfect to practice speaking, listening, and watching. When it comes to progress through play, the key element that seems to grease the wheel is engaging your child in a way that keeps his interest in high gear. And when he is interested, he is also motivated.

I am inspired time and time again by the commitment parents bring to adapting play to a child's individual needs, whether or not that child has special needs. You, as a parent, are first and foremost focused on your child's abilities (rather than disabilities) and you can use these abilities as the starting point for play. If you are a creative thinker, you are constantly brainstorming

The very brain circuits that are activated during play are also activated during joyous, happy moments in our lives, and the more you exercise a brain circuit, the stronger it gets. So letting kids have a good time in play is one of the healthiest things you can do for them."

—Daniel Goleman, PhD
psychologist and author of
Emotional Intelligence and *Social Intelligence*

ways to enhance and adapt your child's play. And, believe me, a can-do, infectious attitude will get passed along to (and absorbed by) your children.

And don't think the opportunities to "seize the play" end here. One of my favorite play traditions has its own special section in this book. I'm talking about Family Game Night, a wonderful way to put your own seal of approval on the importance of play. In the Family Game Night section, you'll find different ideas for activities and games for the entire family to play together. There are silly games, high-energy antics, and quiet kitchen-table games you can play while digging into a big tray of lasagna. You'll find everything you need to plan your very own family tradition of playtime, once a week or once a month. These special times will be remembered long after that rousing round of Follow the Leader is over.

So what are you waiting for? Go forth and seize the play!

Stacking blocks or trying to put one thing inside another, rolling something, or playing in clay or mud or with sticks or boxes—all of those things are teaching toddlers important principles about the three-dimensional physical world."

—Jane M. Healy, PhD
educational psychologist and author of *Your Child's Growing Mind*
and *Failure to Connect: How Computers Affect Our Children's Minds*

TODDLER PLAY

AGES 1 TO 2

Teaching a toddler "how to play" is a little like trying to teach Einstein how to think. Toddlers are wired to play! Every object they encounter becomes a potential toy. Every action they see you do, they imitate as a form of play. Using their hands and arms and moving around is play. Looking inside a box, moving the cardboard flaps back and forth, and dumping its contents on the floor is play. Hearing the songs you sing and listening to the words you read is play. Splashing hands and feet in a dishpan of water is play.

Your toddler's play takes shape as she experiments and explores. Her desire to make things happen directs her play! She pushes a toy car across the wooden floor and it crashes into the couch with an impressive sound and flips up in the air. What sweet satisfaction for a little being who likes to make things happen! The play is fluid and flexible, with one good idea or action leading to another. From your toddler's perspective, the world exists so that she can play, with new and interesting opportunities literally around every corner.

The backstory to all this fun and excitement is that your child is learning and growing with each stroke of play. What an amazing package of self-reliance: I play, therefore I grow.

Here's a snapshot of the specific ways your toddler grows as he plays:

PHYSICAL DEVELOPMENT Large-muscle control, strength, and stamina develop as toddlers walk, run, climb, jump, kick a ball, scoot on ride-on toys, and roll and toss a ball.

Small-muscle control (fingers and hands) and hand–eye coordination improve as toddlers turn knobs, string large beads, play with blocks, use crayons, markers, toy tools, maneuver push toys and pull toys, and transfer an object from one hand to the other with confidence.

INTELLECTUAL DEVELOPMENT A toddler's brain grows and thinking skills develop through play. Toddlers typically learn about cause and effect (if I do x, then y happens); start to understand words and simple instructions; identify objects by pointing (and understand that pictures in a book represent three-dimensional, "real" objects); begin to recognize letters and colors; start to count; experiment and discover how things work (open/close, inside/outside, etc.); and build memory by recognizing stories, songs, and rhymes.

SOCIAL/EMOTIONAL DEVELOPMENT Toddlers develop important social skills as they play. They learn that a conversation consists of listening and talking (and taking turns); to use words to

I think the conclusion we've come to is that people are really a baby's best playmate, and unhurried, sensitive interactions are the best stimulation for the developing brain."

—Ross Thompson, PhD
professor of psychology at University of California, Davis

express their wants and needs; to imitate the actions of others; to start to feel empathy for others in distress (who are crying); to offer toys to another child as a token of friendship (for brief moments of time).

This book was created with two important, related themes in mind. One, that toddlers are the masters of their own play, inventing their own clever play scenarios, often on the spot. (It's important that you think of the "rules" simply as basic ideas for play, because, once again, teaching a toddler "how to play" is a lot like trying to teach Einstein how to think!) And two, your job as a parent is to support and encourage your child's play. You provide safe toys and supervision, offer toddler-friendly play ideas, and give short demos on how to work the toys, props, games, or materials, simply to get things started or help when things get bogged down.

YOUNGER TODDLER PLAY VS. OLDER TODDLER PLAY

Younger toddlers have very different interests and capabilities than older toddlers. The youngest toddlers are in the early stages of learning to walk; they are trying to gain control over their hands and their toys. These are huge physical tasks, and to a great degree, a young toddler's play is all about mastering these skills. Young toddlers tend to explore most toys and objects by putting them in their mouths. (So you must be diligent about their safety each minute of the day.) In short, these toddlers don't have the same physical or cognitive skills that the older ones have, which is important to keep in mind when selecting toys and activities. Toddlers can get overwhelmed with frustration if given a toy to manipulate that is far beyond their capability. And when toddlers have a meltdown, no one is happy.

> "
> Hands-on, three-dimensional, physical play really matters. Between one and two, already this child can start to invent games. She can figure out new ways to do things; and it's coming from inside her own mind. This is what's very important."
>
> **—Jane M. Healy, PhD**
> educational psychologist and author of *Your Child's Growing Mind* and *Failure to Connect: How Computers Affect Our Children's Minds*

Any toys and play activities that are best suited for older toddlers are noted throughout. Older toddlers typically have better hand–eye coordination, can manipulate toys more easily, have steadier balance, and have a better understanding of language. All of these leaps in skills and abilities open up a whole new way of playing.

THE WELL-STOCKED TODDLER TOY CUPBOARD

Just as any chef needs gadgets and supplies in the kitchen, so too does a toddler need toys, props, and materials for a daily life filled with creative, active play. In the back of this book (page 202), you will find an easy-to-navigate list of age-appropriate toys and household items that are marvelous for freewheeling solo play and playing with others too. The list identifies every single item needed to play every single game or activity in the toddler section.

By no means do you need to go out and buy everything suggested in order for your child to have a happy life of playing. Once you've stocked your toy cupboard with just *several* of the items here, you'll be in a wonderful position to begin new and exciting games to hold your toddler's attention—on the spot. So select a few items, as your budget allows, to start creating your toddler's unplugged toy cupboard!

1

SOLO PLAY

I t's safe to say that your toddler isn't going to be old enough to go play outside by herself anytime soon. For one thing, your child needs your constant supervision; for another, she loves to be near you. But she will still be engaged in her own version of solo play, exploring and directing her play, independently, for brief moments each day.

There are two types of solo play for toddlers covered in this section of the book. The first is what I call "Busy-Body Play." The play ideas in this category are perfect for the many occasions when you need a few minutes of concentration to make dinner or work at your desk while your toddler plays happily nearby. (Or perhaps you're looking for a way to keep your child occupied in a waiting room or on a plane.) These games require very simple, basic props or toys, only minimal setup, and can typically be played in one designated play area.

The second category of solo play in this section is called "Spontaneous Play." This type of play is more freewheeling and self-directed; it unfolds naturally as your child explores toys or simple props. With this type of play, your child is on the go, moving from place to place as she investigates and plays. She may pick up a baby doll and begin to feed the baby a bottle and a minute later discover a shoebox across the room that gets incorporated into this ad-lib style of play. Self-directed play is ideal for the times when your child can enjoy freedom to move about, from one area to the next, and decide on her own what to play and how long to play it.

BUSY-BODY PLAY AT HOME

Sometimes a child can become bored and restless when he sees your attention wandering away from him. These activities are designed to captivate your child's attention for a few minutes while you are busy with a task only a few feet away. To get things started, give your toddler a quick demo or show him one or two good ideas for solo play. Many times he will begin by copying you before discovering other ways to play on his own. With busy-body play, he will be using hands and fingers and feet and toes, his eyes and ears and thinking skills too. Of course these activities keep your child busy while you work, but each activity was designed first and foremost to delight and entertain your toddler and put his curiosity and capabilities to work. Most of these play ideas incorporate familiar toys or household items, but offer specific play possibilities that are interesting or challenging to your toddler.

Toddlers like to be where the action is, which means they naturally gravitate to the kitchen, where there is a buzz of excitement a significant part of each day. Let them join in! The kitchen floor or table can be easily transformed into an ideal place for toddler play. Just gather up a few of the simple props and toys used for the games in the following pages (many of which you can find right in your kitchen cupboard), show your child how the game works, and then let your child take over from there. As he explores, your child will enjoy your occasional encouragement, and you will have the pleasure of watching a joyful toddler at play. It's a recipe for cozy, casual, comfortable fun that makes for a happy play routine and wonderful memories too.

KITCHEN SOCCER

AGE:
1–2 years

CATEGORY:
Solo Play/
Busy-Body
at Home

**NUMBER OF
CHILDREN:**
One

* SAFETY ALERT
Be certain to
use plastic
Wiffle golf balls
(or Ping-Pong
balls) rather than
hard, regulation
golf balls.

*Place a laundry basket on its side, propped up
against the wall in the kitchen, to create several
rolling and tossing games that are just right for
toddlers.*

Materials

▸ Pack of plastic Wiffle golf balls*

▸ Unbreakable mixing bowl

▸ medium- to large-size plastic laundry basket

Setup

Place all of the Wiffle balls in the bowl. Put the
laundry basket on its side on the floor, propped
up against the wall or cupboards. (The basket
now resembles a soccer goal.) Squat down to
your toddler's height and give your child a
quick demonstration: Bounce the ball on the
floor about 20 inches away from the basket and
watch it bounce inside the goal. (If you use a
square, plastic mesh laundry basket, the ball
will be less likely to bounce back out.)

Play

Position your toddler 2 to 3 feet away from the
basket, and place the bowl of balls nearby. As
you've demonstrated, the player gives each
ball a hearty bounce and watches as it bounces
into the basket to score a goal. When all the
balls have been bounced inside the goal one
by one, your toddler gathers the balls up, puts
them back into the bowl, and starts over again.

If you're feeling particularly energetic, you can call out "Two points!" every time your toddler bounces a ball into the basket—or just give your nerves a break and let him play on his own!

2 ROMPER ROLL

Set up the laundry basket in the same way described above, but have your child sit on the floor 2 to 3 feet away to roll (rather than bounce) a small- or medium-size ball into the basket. Part of his time will be spent rolling the ball, and part of his time will be spent retrieving it (or chasing after it if it meanders around the room) before sitting back down to roll it again.

> **"**
>
> Play is so important to healthy brain development, not just later in life, but starting very early in babyhood. Why? Because play is what allows kids to manipulate their environment. And how you manipulate your environment is about how you begin to take control, how you begin to develop your senses, how you view the world."
>
> **—Kenneth Ginsburg, MD**
> pediatrician and coauthor of the AAP report on
> *The Importance of Play in Promoting Healthy Child Development and Maintaining Strong Parent-Child Bonds*

WHERE CAN I FIND BEANBAGS?

Toddler-safe beanbags can be purchased at teacher supply or educational supply stores. You'll find sturdy round or square canvas beanbags decorated with colors, numbers, and alphabet letters. These can be used for tossing and are also great during the preschool years for games involving colors, numbers, and letters.

3 **BEANBAG BASKET TOSS**

For older toddlers (nearing thirty-six months), set up the laundry basket in the same way described in the previous activity. Create a "tossing line" on the floor by placing a long piece of painter's tape (or masking tape) across the kitchen floor a short distance away from the laundry basket. Give your child a bowl of toddler-safe beanbags and challenge her to toss each of the beanbags inside the goal (laundry basket).

TUNNEL TUBE

AGE:
1–2 years

CATEGORY:
Solo Play/
Busy-Body
at Home

**NUMBER OF
CHILDREN:**
One

*This simple downhill rolling game involves
a cookie sheet, a towel, a short mailing tube,
and Wiffle balls—no baking involved!*

Materials

▶ Bath towel

▶ Metal cookie sheet

▶ Cardboard mailing tube
(18 to 20 inches long works best)

▶ Duct tape

▶ Invisible tape

▶ Pack of plastic Wiffle golf balls

▶ Plastic sandbox bucket with handle

Setup

Fold the towel in half lengthwise and then roll
it up tightly, like a fruit roll-up. Place the rolled
towel on top of the cookie sheet and slide it to
one end. (This creates the "lift" for one end
of the mailing tube to create a tube-slide for
the ball.) Place the cardboard mailing tube
lengthwise on the cookie sheet, with one end
propped up on the towel, as shown on the next
page.

Secure the high end of the tube in place
using a big piece of duct tape. Tape the other
end of the tube to the cookie sheet using the
invisible tape (to avoid sticky residue after
cleanup). Dump all of the Wiffle balls into the
bucket. Place the cookie sheet on the floor.

Play

Show your toddler how to insert one ball into the high end of the tube, listen to it roll, and watch it come out the other end. Let your child play on her own, taking one ball after another from the bucket and dropping it into the tube. For added excitement, place the cookie sheet (with tube attached) on the seat of a sturdy kitchen chair, place a roasting pan on the floor underneath, and watch as some of the balls bounce inside the pan and others bounce onto the floor. Finding all the balls scattered around the room and putting them back in the bucket is part of the fun.

THE KIDS' CUPBOARD

Toddlers love having their very own kitchen cupboard. And you will love that it can be filled with safe playthings for solo and busy-body play. Ideally, this should be a low cupboard that your child can open and close herself while you work in the kitchen nearby. For toddlers, dragging all the gadgets out of the cupboard is like hunting for a treasure, and experimenting with the objects themselves is a captivating form of wizardry. This serious toddler science consists of stacking containers, putting one item inside the other, putting lids on and taking them off, and seeing what noise can be made with pots and pans. Here are some toddler-safe playthings to include in your kids' cupboard. (Remember to add new gadgets and toys to the cupboard from time to time to spice things up a bit.)

- Cake pans
- Cardboard egg cartons
- Dish towels
- Funnel
- Measuring cups and spoons
- Metal or plastic mixing bowls (stacking)
- Metal roasting pan
- Muffin tins
- Unbreakable plates and cups
- Plastic buckets and tubs (with lids)
- Plastic colander
- Plastic empty squeeze bottles (mustard, ketchup, or syrup)*
- Plastic water bottles*
- Plastic yogurt containers with lids (large)
- Pots and pans with lids

* SAFETY ALERT: Remove small lids or caps to prevent choking hazard.

5 | JOB-JAR

AGE:
2 years

CATEGORY:
Solo Play/
Busy-Body
at Home

**NUMBER OF
CHILDREN:**
One

One of toddlers' favorite types of play is imitating grown-up chores. Create a Job-Jar filled with toddler-friendly cleanup ideas and you'll be surprised by how playful chores can be.

Materials

▸ Marker

▸ Colored construction paper

▸ Giant plastic jar with a lid

▸ Washcloth or dish towel

Setup

Think of a few toddler-safe cleanup or setup ideas that your child can do in the kitchen with you there. Jobs may range from washing the outside of the fridge or kitchen cupboards with a damp washcloth to dusting the kitchen chairs or baseboards (steer clear of feather dusters, as feathers have an uncanny way of winding up in toddlers' noses). Write one job on each piece of paper and fold it in half. Put the papers in the jar.

Play

Pull one piece of paper from the jar and read the chore out loud. Give a quick demonstration of what needs to be done, and give your child a damp washcloth (or dish towel) for the job. Let him improvise his own special way to do this chore. (And remember: This is playtime, so keep the focus on fun rather than spotless cleaning!)

6 PILLOWCASE SURPRISE

AGE:
1–2 years

CATEGORY:
Solo Play/
Busy-Body
at Home

**NUMBER OF
CHILDREN:**
One

Toddlers are delighted to discover toys and objects hidden inside something else. Scour your kitchen cupboard for containers and other safe kitchen gadgets to explore.

Materials

▸ Pillowcase or 6–10 athletic socks (adult size)

▸ Wooden blocks and/or

▸ Plastic toys and/or

▸ Plastic lids and/or

▸ Plastic measuring cups and/or a large plastic bowl

Setup for younger toddlers

Young toddlers are still trying to gain mastery over their hands and fingers, so you'll use a large pillowcase, rather than a sock, for their version of this game. Put 10 to 12 toddler-safe mystery items in the bottom of the pillowcase.

Play

Your younger toddlers looks through the pillowcase to see what he can find. He might pull one item out at a time; he might dump the contents on the floor. This is a great way of holding your child's attention, especially if you put brand-new or unknown toddler-safe items in the pillowcase.

Setup for older toddlers

For your older toddler, gather up 6 to 10 clean, adult-size athletic socks. Hide one toddler-safe mystery object or toy in each sock by pushing it down firmly into the toe. Once you have filled all the socks with one mystery item each, toss them in the giant bowl.

Play

Challenge your child to find all the mystery items by wiggling them out of the socks. Or, she can guess what's inside by reaching in and touching the object. If wiggling her hand inside the sock is too difficult, your child may discover she can hold on to the toe section of the sock and spill the contents out onto the floor quite easily. After all the mystery objects have come out, line them up in a row so your child can give a little commentary about what she has found.

66

It's not so easy being a toddler. They're weaker than us, they're slower than us, they can't speak as well. They feel like they're losing all day long. They just want to win a few. And what works the best with toddlers is to allow them to win little tiny things just to feel triumphant in little moments all throughout the day."

—Harvey Karp, MD
pediatrician and author of *The Happiest Toddler on the Block*

TODDLER-SAFE PLAYTIME

A parent's *number one* job is to keep their child safe. With a toddler in the family, this job requires planning, commitment, and constant supervision. Though curiosity is a wonderful thing, remember that toddlers don't yet understand the concept of danger, so you must be their eyes and ears to keep them safe. (Clearly convey safety rules and the need for constant supervision to all of your childcare providers and teenage babysitters too.) The very first step is to take a realistic look at your surroundings, with an eye toward your toddler's capabilities, reach, and interests. Here are some general guidelines to keep in mind regarding toddler play and safety:

▶ Toddlers need constant adult supervision when they play indoors and outdoors.

▶ Remove or cover all furniture with sharp edges or corners.

▶ Remove small tables and chairs that can easily tip over.

▶ Keep older siblings' toys and games with small parts out of reach.

▶ Carefully supervise all play that involves water, including buckets and tubs of water.

▶ Keep safety latches on cabinets that store chemicals, cleaning supplies, or medicine.

▶ Install safety gates to protect your child from falls on stairs.

▶ Balloons pose a serious choking hazard; keep them away from toddlers.

MUFFIN SORTER

AGE:
1–2 years

CATEGORY:
Solo Play/
Busy-Body
at Home

**NUMBER OF
CHILDREN:**
One

Just pinching items with fingers, picking them up, and putting them inside little containers is pure and exhilarating play for toddlers.

Materials

▸ Assorted toddler-safe objects for sorting: plastic Wiffle golf balls; giant pop beads; tiny colorful sock-balls (made using 1 or 2 toddler-size socks); plastic or wooden toy figures or animals

▸ Unbreakable mixing bowl

▸ Muffin tin

Setup

Place all of the objects in the plastic bowl. Put the muffin tin and bowl on the floor next to your child. The object of the game is to place the various materials inside the muffin compartments, take them out, put them in again, and perhaps to dump the contents onto the floor and watch the action as the items scatter. So simple, yet so satisfying! (If your child seems more enamored with taking things out than with arranging them in the muffin tins, start by filling each muffin compartment with objects and place the empty bowl nearby.)

8 | SCRUB-A-DUB

AGE:
1–2 years

CATEGORY:
Solo Play/
Busy-Body
at Home

**NUMBER OF
CHILDREN:**
One

* SAFETY ALERT

Always supervise
toddlers when
they are playing
with water. Also,
if your child likes
to put things
in his mouth,
sponges can
pose a choking
hazard, so use
a washcloth
instead.

*Toddlers love to imitate what you do, and they
love to play around in water. Mix these two
things together for a game of Scrub-a-Dub.*

Materials

▸ Beach towel

▸ Small plastic dishpan

▸ Plastic lids from food containers

▸ Baby-size washcloth (or regular washcloth,
cut into 4 pieces)

Setup

Fold the beach towel in half and place it on
the floor. Put 1 inch of water* in the dishpan
and place the dishpan on top of the towel. Toss
the plastic lids and small washcloth inside the
dishpan.

Play

Young toddlers will enjoy playing around with
the water and plastic lids. Older toddlers will
get a kick out of scrubbing the lids to make
them "really clean."

9 SCRUBBING BABY'S DISHES

Ask your toddler to help you scrub all the
baby utensils while you work in the kitchen.
A little plastic tub with only an inch of water
can provide a good stretch of fun. Put a
collection of safe infant spoons and bowls,
spill-proof infant cups, baby-bottle rings,

and nipples into the water. Provide a small washcloth for soap-free scrubbing!

10 SPOON SCRUB AND SORT

Rummage through your silverware drawer and create an odds-and-ends collection of teaspoons that aren't in use or don't match and designate them for regular Scrub and Sort playtime for your older toddler. Buy an inexpensive plastic utensil organizer with four or five compartments; store these special spoons in the tray in a low cupboard so that your toddler can get to them. Ask your toddler to scrub and sort these spoons for your family while you are in the kitchen working. Fill the small plastic tub with an inch of water and the washcloth and have your child dump all the spoons into the water and give them a scrub. Have a dish towel standing by so he can dry the spoons and place them one by one in the tray's compartments.

11 ROCK SCRUB

Medium to large rocks (the size of a potato) from a creek bank with a vegetable scrubber or large sponge are good fun for a toddler. (Caution: Do not let your child play with small stones or rocks, which could be a choking hazard.)

12   SHAKE, RATTLE-N-ROLL

AGE:
1–2 years

CATEGORY:
Solo Play/
Busy-Body
at Home

**NUMBER OF
CHILDREN:**
One

* SAFETY ALERT

Tennis balls are
not intended
to be tasted
by toddlers, so
provide careful
supervision.

Materials

▸ Plastic tennis-ball container with lid

▸ 3 new tennis balls*

Play

With the three tennis balls inside, secure the
lid on the plastic tube. Children one to two
years old will enjoy placing the tube on its side
on the floor and giving it a shove to see how
far it will roll. They also like shaking the tube
with both hands and listening to the racket the
balls create. Last but not least, lifting off the
lid, dumping the balls on the floor, and chasing
after them makes for excellent sport.

Any object in your household is a toy to a baby.
So you can be doing laundry and sorting socks,
and your child can just be putting the laundry
in and out of the hamper. And you know what?
To a child, that's a perfectly fun way to learn up
and down, and high and low, and in and out, and
eventually reds and whites, and counting."

—Maureen O'Brien, MD
child development specialist and author of
Watch Me Grow: I'm One-Two-Three

13 | DUCKIE-DIP

AGE:
2 years

CATEGORY:
Solo Play/
Busy-Body
at Home

**NUMBER OF
CHILDREN:**
One

* SAFETY ALERT
Stepping on
a Ping-Pong
ball can create
sharp edges and
points that could
become a hazard
for children.
Supervise so
as to avoid any
hazards.

*Rubber duckies from the bathtub find their way
into the kitchen in this game.*

Materials

▶ Beach towel

▶ Plastic dishpan

▶ Floating tub toys, such as plastic ducks or
Ping-Pong balls*

▶ Small kitchen strainer or tiny fishnet
(used for fish tanks)

▶ Large plastic food-storage container or
giant plastic mixing bowl

Setup

Fold the beach towel in half and place it on the
floor or kitchen table. Put 2 inches of water in
the dishpan and place it on top of the towel.
Add the floating ducks or Ping-Pong balls to
the dishpan.

Play

Give your child the strainer to use as a net,
and see how many ducks or balls he can catch.
The items caught go into the mixing bowl.
When all the critters have been caught, the
player plops them back in the water and starts
all over again.

HALLWAY BAG-BALL

AGE:
1–2 years

CATEGORY:
Solo Play/
Busy-Body
at Home

**NUMBER OF
CHILDREN:**
One

* SAFETY ALERT
Because of
the fuzz and
dye used in
manufacturing,
tennis balls are
only appropriate
for children who
no longer put
things in their
mouth.

Use toddler-safe
balls to avoid
choking hazard.

*The next time the cashier asks, "Paper or plastic?"
pick the paper sack so your toddler can play
Hallway Bag-Ball!*

Materials

▸ Paper grocery bag
▸ Plastic balls or tennis balls*

Setup

Have your toddler sit on any uncarpeted floor.
Fully open the paper grocery bag and place
it on the floor on one of its long sides, several
yards away from your child. (Give the bag a
little stretch to keep it open.) Squat down next
to your child and roll the ball so that it goes
inside the paper bag.

Play

Once your child sees how to play, she'll simply
roll the balls and retrieve them from inside the
bag. Both parts of the game, hitting the target
and retrieving the balls, are equally enjoyable.

THE HONORABLE, HUMBLE PAPER BAG

A paper grocery bag is a versatile prop for toddler play. It can be a lightweight, carryall container for your toddler, ideal for moving a favorite toy from place to place. It is easily transformed into a hiding place for peekaboo items—close the flap, Teddy is gone, open the flap and he appears once again. A stiff new grocery bag placed on its side becomes a goal for a ball rolling along the floor (see Hallway Bag-Ball on the opposite page). Or remove the bottom of the bag with a pair of scissors and place it on its side with a bit of invisible tape and you've created a terrific tunnel. (Zoom a push-and-go car through the tunnel and your child will squeal with delight; roll a ball through the tunnel once, and then let your child take over.)

15 | BOX BALL

Question: What's thin, flat, and inanimate and can be transformed into a ball with the squeeze of two hands? Answer: a piece of paper!

Materials

QUICK & EASY

▶ Medium-size cardboard box
  (or large plastic colander)

▶ Sheets of colored construction paper
  or copy paper*

Setup

Set up the cardboard box a few feet away from your child.

Play

Your child crumples the colored paper into balls, tosses the balls into the cardboard box to score a basket, and dumps all the paper balls back onto the floor to start all over again.

16 OUTDOOR BOX BALL

For older toddlers, create your own game of outdoor Box Ball for a few minutes of high-energy fun. First, work with your child to make an assortment of paper balls; then, find an appropriate container to act as the catching basket (a kitchen colander, child's sand bucket, plastic sieve, or wastebasket all work well). You hold the container, your child tosses the ball in your direction, and you chase and catch it in your container. For more paper-ball fun out in the yard, create a tossing line on the lawn with masking tape (roll out the tape, sticky side down, pressing your feet as you go to secure it). Stand back a few feet and toss the balls over the line.

BOX PLAY

Introduce your toddler to a cardboard box and she's likely to climb inside for a test drive! Cardboard storage boxes are wonderful crawl spaces, scooting machines, and receptacles for flying beanbags. Gift boxes can become a holding place for outdoor treasures like shells and leaves. Recycled pudding, cake, muffin, or cereal boxes make realistic props for "grocery store" play. Use the lid of a shirt box to create a zoo for plastic animals, a house for plastic people, a truck to slide across the carpet . . .

EDIBLE FINGER PAINT

AGE:
1–2 years

CATEGORY:
Solo Play/
Busy-Body
at Home

**NUMBER OF
CHILDREN:**
One

NOTE
If your child prefers to sit at the kitchen table, you can also contain the mess by placing the edible finger paint in the middle of a cookie sheet with sides.

Here's a way to allow your child the pleasure of smearing edible finger paint around and around, with easy cleanup built into the play.

Materials
▸ Small mixing bowl (unbreakable)
▸ Flour
▸ Water
▸ High chair (with plastic tray)
▸ Tiny drop of food coloring (optional)

Setup
In a small mixing bowl, stir a small quantity of flour and some warm water together until the substance reaches the consistency of runny pudding or baby food. Add a drop of food coloring if you want color. Allow the mixture to cool before your child plays with it.

Play
Place your toddler in her high chair and snap the tray in place. Dump the contents of the goop on the tray and let your child finger paint to her heart's content. Place newspapers on the floor beneath the high chair for easy cleanup.

BAKE ME A CAKE

AGE:
2 years

CATEGORY:
Solo Play/
Busy-Body
at Home

**NUMBER OF
CHILDREN:**
One

* SAFETY ALERT

Please supervise
your child
carefully so
that none of
the ingredients
create a choking
hazard. This food
play activity is
about mixing
and stirring (the
goop should
not be eaten)
and may not
be appropriate
for younger
toddlers (who
put everything
in their mouths).

*Can you tolerate a little orchestrated mess today?
If so, here's an activity that is goopy fun for
toddlers!*

Materials*

▸ Water

▸ Small plastic tub (margarine, for example)

▸ Flour or cornmeal

▸ Spoon

▸ Small size measuring cup(s)

▸ Toy cake pan or loaf pan

Setup

Put your child in her high chair. Put about
½ cup water in the plastic tub. Add several
tablespoons of flour or cornmeal to make a
soupy, runny mixture—the cake batter! Be
prepared for some spills.

Play

Hand your child a spoon and ask him to mix up
a "cake" with these goopy ingredients. Mixing
is good fun and so is spooning the goop into
the cake pan using the small measuring cup.

PIZZA-PIZZA

AGE:
2 years

CATEGORY:
Solo Play/
Busy-Body
at Home

**NUMBER OF
CHILDREN:**
One

* SAFETY ALERT
This activity is
not appropriate
for younger
toddlers or
toddlers who
may choke on
the ingredients.

NOTE
This pizza is not
intended to be
cooked, but can
be eaten.

*A toddler-inspired pizza pie that may or may not
be eaten but is deliciously fun to make.*

Materials*

▶ Dry, toddler-safe cereal

▶ Raisins (soft), or other toddler-safe foods

▶ Small plastic bowls

▶ Waxed paper

▶ Small cardboard pizza box

▶ ¼ cup flavored yogurt

▶ Flour tortilla

▶ Spoon

Setup

Set up the pizza-making station at the kitchen
table or by spreading a tablecloth on the floor
to create a toddler-friendly work space. Put
a few tablespoons of cereal and raisins, to be
used as "pizza toppings," in each of the bowls.
Put a piece of waxed paper in the bottom of the
pizza box. Spread about ¼ cup yogurt on the
flour tortilla, put it inside the pizza box, and
hand it to the "pizza chef."

Play

Your toddler uses the spoon to spread the "sauce" around on the pizza a little more. Then he adds the pizza toppings one at a time. (Provide only healthy, toddler-safe "toppings" for this activity so that you don't have to worry if your toddler eats as he plays.) When he finishes his pizza, your child may close the box and play pizza delivery next.

BUSY-BODY PLAY HIGH AND LOW

Many of the busy-body activities in this book can be adapted for the high chair or the playpen so you can keep your child in one place for a few minutes while you work nearby. My friend Kiki calls her child's high chair his "desk" when he wants to play "office"; at other times it is miraculously transformed into a chef's "table" when her child wants to play "cook." This is a splendid way to keep your child close, within eyesight, and safe.

WHY "NO TV OR VIDEOS" IS BEST FOR YOUR TODDLER

The AAP recommends that screen time (and digital media use) for children under two years of age should be very limited and allowed only when an adult is standing by to co-view, talk, and teach. I usually want to know why when I hear a rule like this, and perhaps you do too. Here are some concrete reasons why these AAP recommendations make perfect sense for toddlers:

▹ Toddlers are wired to be active learners who explore and experiment through play. The passive viewing encouraged by a video is quite different from the hands-on approach to which toddler brains are naturally prone.

▹ Toddlers want and need to develop their physical selves through movement (it's the path to large- and small-muscle development). Television and video viewing is sedentary and discourages the very movement their growing bodies crave. (The AAP says that childhood obesity is clearly linked to lack of physical play and exercise.)

▹ Hands-on active play promotes growth for the whole child (physically, socially, emotionally, and intellectually). When toddlers play physically—with balls, blocks, and toys—they develop thinking skills too. By hauling blocks around or stacking them, for example, they begin to understand cause and effect and discover the properties of matter, shape, and size. Social skills come into active play as well; toddlers learn to get along with others and resolve conflicts as they play.

- Toddlers are wired to learn language through everyday interactions. Language acquisition relies upon having many spontaneous, back-and-forth conversations with others. A parent asks a question and the toddler answers, which causes the parent to say something more. This two-way conversation is very gratifying to a toddler. She asks for more milk and she gets it. Machines project sound in your child's direction, but even a toddler quickly learns that you can't have a true conversation with a television. When toddlers play with parents, language blossoms.

- Toddlers practice patience and learn to tolerate frustration as they play. The boy who gets mildly upset when his three-block tower tumbles down has a chance to persevere in the face of a disappointment. He tries again and again and may eventually get the blocks to do just what he wants. This lesson of perseverance plants a seed in the toddler's mind: mastering something new takes time. Many videos, with their alluring special effects and fast-paced action, send quite a different message to toddlers, and educators worry that they set the stage for a shortened attention span and the expectation of instant gratification.

- Toddlers form expectations and habits through their everyday routines. When your child has the freedom to play and explore with open-ended toys that allow for many ways to play, he comes to believe that he can make things happen through his own actions. This is a powerful discovery with lifelong repercussions.

BUSY-BODY PLAY ON-THE-GO

Keeping your toddler busy in your own home is one thing; passing time happily while you are out and about, especially when there is waiting involved, is quite another. Because toddlers are so curious, they often want to run around and explore any new and exciting environment. In order to compete with the excitement of a new place, you must carry a few new and exciting playthings in the diaper bag to hold your child's attention while you wait. On the other hand, there may be days (and environments) when your child will seek the comfort of a familiar, soothing activity while you wait. The best plan is to be prepared with props for both situations. Here are some portable games that may serve you well when you find yourself in the waiting mode in various settings away from home.

20

CREATIVITY IN THE EXAMINING ROOM

PARENT TIP

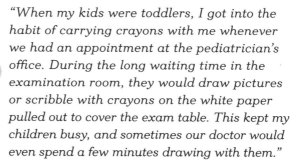

"When my kids were toddlers, I got into the habit of carrying crayons with me whenever we had an appointment at the pediatrician's office. During the long waiting time in the examination room, they would draw pictures or scribble with crayons on the white paper pulled out to cover the exam table. This kept my children busy, and sometimes our doctor would even spend a few minutes drawing with them."

—**Peggy from Maryland**

SCRIBBLE-SCRABBLE NOTEBOOK

AGE:
1–2 years

CATEGORY:
Solo Play/
Busy-Body
On-the-Go

**NUMBER OF
CHILDREN:**
One

Toddlers love having their very own notebook with pages to flip and a plastic crayon-filled pocket.

Materials

▸ ½-inch thick three-ring binder with clear plastic sleeve on cover

▸ Notebook paper for three-ring binder

▸ Plastic (zip-style) pencil pouch with three holes to fit inside three-ring binder

▸ Toddler-size crayons

▸ 8½-by-11-inch piece of paper with a color photo of your toddler (print this photo from your computer or take a 4-by-6-inch photo to your local copy center to make a color copy on 8½-by-11-inch paper)

Setup

Fill the notebook with paper, put crayons in the plastic pencil pouch, and insert the 8½-by-11-inch photo of your child into the clear sleeve on the front of the notebook. Keep the notebook in your tote bag for whenever boredom strikes!

Play

This is a special notebook that should only be brought out for drawing and scribbling when you are on the go. Your child may prefer to do all her own coloring, or she may like opening the notebook so that you can draw on one page and she can draw on the other. Follow her lead.

POLKA-DOT HAT TO-GO

AGE:
1–2 years

CATEGORY:
Solo Play/
Busy-Body
On-the-Go

**NUMBER OF
CHILDREN:**
One

*Work with your toddler to put sticky "dots"
(or shapes) all over a clear sherbet tub and
you've created a colorful hat to wear while
waiting. The finished hat is not much for
grown-up eyes to look at, but it sure is cool
to make!*

Materials

▶ Color dot stickers (available at office supply stores,
or use scissors to create your own dots and shapes
from the sticky parts of Post-it notes)

▶ Empty sherbet tub with lid

Setup

Put the stickers inside the plastic tub, snap
on the lid, and toss in your diaper bag.

Play for younger toddlers

Remove the lid from the tub and take the
stickers out. Turn the plastic tub upside down
on the floor, peel off a sticker, and apply it to
the surface of the tub. Quickly hand another
sticker to your child and show him how to stick
it on the tub. Continue to hand stickers to your
child as he decorates the entire "hat." If you
run out of room on the hat, hand your child the
lid and let him decorate that as well.

Play for older toddlers

Your older toddler may be able to peel the
stickers off the sheet of paper on his own, and
that action becomes part of the play. (If your

child has trouble peeling, use your fingernails to loosen just the top edge of all the stickers on the page.) Older toddlers may take time to create some sort of "design"—using all the red dots on one section and then applying all the blue dots to another, for example.

23   HOLD ON TO YOUR COUPONS

"I rescued my husband's worn-out leather wallet from the wastebasket a few months ago and created 'money' to put inside it by cutting colorful coupons from the pharmacy insert in the Sunday paper. I keep this wallet in my purse for my twenty-one-month-old son, Joshua, to play with whenever we find ourselves waiting someplace. In a sit-down restaurant, I'll pull out Josh's wallet and he has a good time dumping all the money on the table and sorting through it. Then I help him put it in a stack and fit it back inside the wallet. It's amazing how much amusement he's gotten out of this old, beat-up wallet."

—Lynn from Ohio

SCARF MAGIC

AGE:
1–2 years

CATEGORY:
Solo Play/
Busy-Body
On-the-Go

**NUMBER OF
CHILDREN:**
One

* SAFETY ALERT
Supervise
toddlers carefully
so they do not
get tangled in
the scarves.

TIP
If your child has
trouble finding
the end of the
scarf, knot one
corner of each
scarf before you
stuff it in the cup.
Then instruct her
to "find the knot."
Your child may
also enjoy stuffing
and mashing all
the scarves back
into the cup,
which will extend
the play.

*Long, silky scarves stuffed inside a big cup
appear to grow longer and longer with every
tug. It really looks like magic!*

Materials

▶ Scissors (for adult use only)

▶ Large, rigid plastic or paper beverage "to go" cup
with sturdy plastic lid

▶ 3 or 4 long, narrow silk scarves*

Setup

Cut a big hole (the size of a silver dollar) in
the lid of the large to-go cup. Tie the scarves
together end to end (by knotting the corners)
to create one humongous, long scarf. Stuff the
giant scarf into the cup, leaving one end of the
scarf on top. Put the lid on the cup and toss
it into your diaper bag for the moment your
toddler gets a little bit impatient or bored.

Play

When your child is ready to play, thread the
end of the first scarf through the big hole in
the top of the lid. Help your toddler grab the
end of the scarf and begin pulling it out of the
cup. You will need to hold the lid in place while
she pulls the long scarf all the way out of the
cup. Your toddler will delight in the perception
that her tugging action seems to make the
scarf "grow" right before her very eyes.

25 SIMPLE MAGIC

For a simpler version, remove the cup lid and layer three or four scarves on top of one another inside so your child can search for and pull out each scarf from the cup one by one.

26 MOMMY'S CART

PARENT
TIP

"My son is two and a half and loves to go grocery shopping with me—as long as he gets to push his own grocery cart through the aisles. I take his toy cart along and he proudly pushes it around the store while I push the regular cart. He's old enough to understand the basic idea that only Mom is allowed to get items off the shelf, so I hand him any item that is small enough to handle (and unbreakable), and he puts these items in his cart. When there is a meat item or something messy, I simply say, 'This is meat for Mommy's cart,' and he's perfectly content. When it's time to check out, we head for the lane without candy, and I always let him push his cart up to the register in front of my cart. Then he hands me each item from his cart and I place it on the conveyer belt. He's a bit slow in doing this, which works out fine, because I have time to unload one or two items from my cart in between his items and we check out pretty quickly."

—**Diana from Connecticut**

LUNCH-BOX ART

AGE:
1–2 years

CATEGORY:
Solo Play/
Busy-Body
On-the-Go

**NUMBER OF
CHILDREN:**
One

* SAFETY ALERT
Supervise
your toddler
carefully so
that she doesn't
put any of the
art supplies or
materials in
her mouth.

*Waiting for the food to arrive at a restaurant is
one of the more difficult waiting times for a child.
But it doesn't have to be!*

Materials*

▸ Lunch box

▸ Large crayons

▸ Stack of plain white copy paper (rolled width-wise
   and secured with a rubber band) or 4-by-6-inch
   index cards

▸ Roll of invisible tape

▸ Sheets of round, colorful stickers
   (available at office supply stores)

Setup

Pack a lunch box full of simple, toddler-safe
art supplies that your child can pull out during
those waiting times.

Play

Let your child scribble, draw, and sticker right
at the table, and then stow it away easily when
the food comes.

SLOT MACHINE

AGE:
1–2 years

CATEGORY:
Solo Play/
Busy-Body
On-the-Go

**NUMBER OF
CHILDREN:**
One

Breathe new life into a ho-hum deck of playing cards to create this portable coffee-can game.

Materials

▶ Scissors and duct tape (for adult use only)
▶ Empty coffee can with lid
▶ Deck of playing cards

Setup

Use scissors to cut a slit in the lid of the coffee can long enough so that one playing card can slip through. Use small pieces of duct tape to cover the inside rim of the can to cover any potentially sharp edges. Put the deck of cards inside the coffee can, put the lid on, and put this "toy" in your diaper bag.

Play

Remove the deck of cards from the can and replace the lid. Hand your child one card at a time and ask him to put each card through the slot. Once all the cards are in, open the lid and let him dump them out and start all over again. He may play another round on his own.

SPONTANEOUS PLAY

Toddlers are inventors and explorers, and it shows in their play. When your child grabs a new dump truck for the first time, it's as though a little voice inside his brain calls out, "This really is something! How does it work? What can I do with it?" Then your child uses his hands and whole body to answer these questions as he plays. This is what I call "Self-Directed Solo Play." If you join in the play, it's usually best to let your child lead the way—though he may need just a wee bit of a demonstration to see how to manipulate a new toy or object. In that case, you provide a quick how-to, and then let your little play-master invent his own play. Since this style of play is all about exploring in a spontaneous way, many of the play ideas appear without "how-to-play" instructions.

29 | DOLLS

AGE:
1–2 years

CATEGORY:
Solo Play/
Spontaneous

**NUMBER OF
CHILDREN:**
One

A baby doll can be washed and fed and put to bed by your toddler. This is a fun way for your toddler to imitate an adult caring for baby.

Materials

▸ Baby doll

▸ Simple, toddler-safe baby accessories: tiny hairbrush with extra-soft bristles and short round handle; baby bottle; plastic spoon and bowls; tiny toy high chair; baby clothes; shoebox to use as baby bed; baby blanket or dish towel; small plastic tub and damp washcloth (no water needed); doll stroller or tiny plastic wagon

Setup

Assemble a few simple props and give each prop a name. ("Here's a bathtub for baby. Here are baby's bed and blanket.") Show your child how to brush the baby's hair or wash the baby's face with the damp washcloth.

30 THE ART OF REDIRECTION

PARENT TIP

"My two-year-old's favorite word seems to be 'no.' He really seems to get a kick out of saying it! What I try to do, whenever possible, is find the reverse thing that we can say yes to when he digs in his heels with a no. So, for example, if my son does not want to get his coat on when it's time to go outside, I lightheartedly say, 'Yes, you do get to go outside and play when you put your coat on.' Then I enthusiastically add, 'I wonder what fun things we will discover outside together today; maybe a caterpillar, maybe a squirrel, maybe another big red rock.' Usually by this time in the conversation, he's thinking about the outdoor adventures I'm describing and the word 'no' has just faded into the background."

—Rebecca from New Jersey

RIDE A WAGON

AGE:
1–2 years

CATEGORY:
Solo Play/
Spontaneous

**NUMBER OF
CHILDREN:**
One

* SAFETY ALERT
Supervise water
play carefully,
and don't
provide items
that pose a
choking risk to
children who are
prone to putting
things in their
mouths.

Wagons let you transport lots of things from place to place. Indoors, toddlers can fill up a wagon with cars, trucks, blocks, and books. Outdoors, rocks, leaves, dolls, and stuffed animals are taken for a (somewhat bumpy) ride.

Materials

▸ Safe, small (toddler-size) plastic wagon

▸ Assorted items to haul indoors:* blocks, books, assorted plastic food containers and lids, junk mail, all the hats in the house, sock-balls (athletic socks rolled into balls), small cardboard boxes, toddler-safe shoes and sandals

▸ Assorted items to haul outdoors:* large rocks and stones, leaves, water, sand, dirt, measuring cups, floating toys (small ducks, boats, etc.)

Setup

Indoors, designate one low kitchen cupboard to hold all the toddler-safe items for wagon loading. Or add dolls or stuffed animals to transform the wagon into a portable dollhouse or barn. Outdoors, fill the wagon with an inch or two of water* and expect a bit of splashing and wet clothes. Add floating toys and measuring cups for portable water play, or add a washcloth and use the wagon as a "bathtub" for dolls. Create a giant "car wash" for your child's plastic cars, trucks, or plastic balls, with plastic cups for rinsing. Add seashells or rocks that need a good bath, and provide a baby toothbrush for some soap-free scrubbing.

32 BEAT THE BUZZER

"Every weekend, my two children (ages two and three-and-a-half) drag out nearly every toy they own. By the end of the day our home looks like a war zone. I wanted the children to learn to help put all these toys away, so I came up with a 'game' that we play called Beat the Buzzer. Basically, I just announce that it's time to play Beat the Buzzer and get the kitchen timer (which has a rather loud 'buzzer sound' rather than a beep). I give each child a big box to put all their toys in. Playing this cleanup game has taken me out of the nagging role. And our older child enjoys the challenge of trying to get all her toys in the box before the buzzer sounds. My two-year-old son mainly likes to play because his sister is playing, so I have to help him pick up some of his toys so he can 'win' before the buzzer sounds."

—Tom from California

❝

The closer the contact between parent and child at the earliest stages, the better the relationship and the better the outcome for the child."

—John Evans
psychotherapist and author of *Marathon Dads*

33 CARS AND TRUCKS

AGE:
1–2 years

CATEGORY:
Solo Play/
Spontaneous

**NUMBER OF
CHILDREN:**
One

*Toddlers love brightly colored dump trucks,
push-and-go cars, and every transportation
toy in between! After making these easy tunnels
and garages out of shoeboxes, show your toddler
how to zoom her car through a tunnel or park it
in the garage.*

Materials

▶ Shoeboxes and small- to medium-size cardboard boxes

▶ Marker (for adult use only)

▶ Ruler

▶ Scissors (for adult use only)

▶ Toddler-safe plastic or wooden trucks, cars, and trains

Setup

Create a series of "garages" and "tunnels"
for your child's cars and trucks. To make
the tunnels, place a shoebox or a cardboard
box upside down on a table and draw a large

RAMP IT UP!

A large sheet of foam board (poster board with foam backing) makes
a terrific ramp for zooming small cars and trucks down a hill. Prop the
foam board up against your couch or easy chair at an angle. This ramp
will stay in place when positioned on carpeting; if you have a hard
floor, use strips of invisible tape to hold it in place. Stuffed animals
have been known to take a ride down this slippery slide as well.

upside-down *U* in the center of each of the two long sides of the box. (Your *U*s should match up exactly, so use a ruler to make sure.) Use scissors to cut out the tunnel openings. To make a garage, make the same cutout but on only one side of a shoebox. Put the lid on the top of the box so the garage has a dashing roof!

34 STUFFED ANIMAL HOUSE

AGE:
1–2 years

CATEGORY:
Solo Play/
Spontaneous

**NUMBER OF
CHILDREN:**
One

Many children have one special, beloved stuffed animal that plays the role of a quiet, lovable playmate.

Materials

▶ Tablecloth

▶ Stuffed animal(s) and/or plastic (toddler-safe) people or action figures

Optional

▶ Shoebox (bed)

▶ Tea set

▶ Dish towel

Setup

Drape an extra-large tablecloth over one end of the kitchen table or a card table and secure in place, so that it creates a fort or house for the stuffed animal. (Young toddlers may simply enjoy crawling into "Teddy's" house; older toddlers may like outfitting the house with a shoebox for Teddy's bed and plates for Teddy's dinnertime.) Help organize a tea party.

BUMPER BALL

AGE:
1–2 years

CATEGORY:
Solo Play/
Spontaneous

**NUMBER OF
CHILDREN:**
One

*A large plastic ball and two makeshift "bumpers"
on the floor set the stage for brilliant ball play—
rolling the ball and watching it bounce back
each time.*

Materials

▸ 2 cardboard mailing tubes

▸ Roll of painter's tape (or masking tape)

▸ Large, toddler-safe plastic ball with plenty of bounce

Setup

Designate a playing area in the kitchen that
is free from foot traffic. Your child will need
approximately 4 feet of uncluttered floor space
(uncarpeted floor is best) and a wall without
furniture to serve as the "backboard" for play.
Place the two mailing tubes side by side on the
floor, perpendicular to the wall, then angle the
tubes to create a V, with 1 foot of space between
the tube ends near the wall and 2 feet of space
between the tube ends farthest from the wall.
Tape them in place. These create "bumpers"
(similar to those used at the bowling alley for
young bowlers). Provide a quick demo for your
child to start the play: Stand a few feet back
from the bumpers and roll the ball into the V
so that it hits the wall (backboard) and comes
rolling right back to you. Now let your toddler
take over.

BLOCKS

AGE:
1–2 years

CATEGORY:
Solo Play/
Spontaneous

**NUMBER OF
CHILDREN:**
One

Toddlers love to pile up blocks, knock them down, put them in a wagon, and haul them around (and sometimes they stack them up to make a fine tower too). Once they begin to show an interest in pretend play, blocks can become a wonderful prop for more elaborate scenarios.

Materials

▸ Toddler-safe blocks (wooden, cardboard, interlocking plastic)

▸ Small plastic wagon

Setup

Show your younger toddler how to stack blocks end to end or on top of one another in stacks of two or three. Show your older toddler how to create simple patterns using the different colors. Leave a plastic wagon (or a cardboard box if you don't have one) nearby in case they're inspired to transport the blocks.

66

Stacking blocks or trying to put one thing inside another, rolling something, or playing in clay or mud or with sticks or boxes—all of those things are teaching toddlers important principles about the three-dimensional physical world."

—Jane M. Healy, PhD
educational psychologist and author of
Your Child's Growing Mind and *Failure to Connect:
How Computers Affect Our Children's Minds*

RIDE-ON TOYS

AGE:
1–2 years

CATEGORY:
Solo Play/
Spontaneous

**NUMBER OF
CHILDREN:**
One

Toddlers are keen on scooting from place to place on their ride-on toy; unknown to them, it's a marvelous way to build muscles and develop coordination. If yours needs a little encouragement and you happen to have an office chair handy, you might just want to display the principle of scooting and riding!

Materials

▶ Plastic or wooden ride-on toys that your child propels by scooting his feet. Here are a few of my favorites: fire truck, farm tractor (seat lifts up to reveal farm animals inside), motor scooter (nonelectric), jeep, race car, plane, school bus (seat lifts up to reveal plastic people inside), pony

"

There are so many things that you can do that encourage play for your child. And then to see the child come up with things that you hadn't even thought of; that's the best of all!"

—Fred Rogers
Emmy award–winning creator and host of
Mister Rogers' Neighborhood

THE JOYS OF PULLING AND PUSHING

I'm talking about pull toys and push toys—terrific fun for toddlers. Pull toys are exciting for older toddlers who have mastered walking and are able to maneuver toys around furniture and doorways. For younger toddlers, large, sturdy ride-on toys with a high, upright handle or grab bar in back can be used to help them walk. Other, smaller push toys are just plain fun to zoom around with—and "just plain fun" is a concept any parent and child can get behind. Here are a few of my favorite pull and push toys:

Pull Toys

▶ Classic pull-along telephone

▶ Duck on a string (waddles and quacks)

▶ Pull-along wooden block set (in wooden wagon)

▶ Pull-along wooden stacking animals

▶ Train on a string

Push Toys

▶ Doll stroller

▶ Mini (plastic) grocery cart

▶ Mini (plastic) lawn mower

▶ Mini (plastic) vacuum cleaner

▶ Musical roll-along toy with safe, rounded handle (so child won't get hurt if she falls)

▶ Popcorn popper

▶ Push-along trains, cars, trucks, boats, tractors, airplanes

▶ Push-and-go vehicles (depress the plastic passenger and the car zooms forward)

▶ Wooden giraffe walker (shape sorter attached)

PRETEND PLAY & ROLE-PLAY

Children one to two years old are just starting to show an interest in role-play and pretending. Your toddler may imitate the things she sees you doing—talking on the phone, stirring a spoon in a pan, feeding the dog, or mowing the lawn. As your toddler moves from the second to third year of life, her imitations and pretending may become much more involved. Your thirty-month-old daughter, for example, may play "grocery store" by placing boxes and cartons in a toy shopping cart, opening her purse to find money, or unloading her groceries at the kitchen table.

Here are some favorite play activities that incorporate imitation, role-play, or imagination. Toddlers love to imitate and pretend in their own way, so all the help your child may need to get started is having a few good props and toys available. Note that because children one to two years old typically have a different way of "pretending" than children two to three years old, you'll find play ideas for each of these age groups in this section.

---

38 | MAILBOX

AGE:
1–2 years

CATEGORY:
Solo Play/
Pretend

**NUMBER OF
CHILDREN:**
One

Mail is just one of those life mysteries that fascinates children. It's a winning combination of the written word, an adult in a uniform, and a little box with a now-you-see-it-now-you-don't slot.

Materials

▶ Scissors (for adult use only)

▶ Cardboard shoebox (with lid)

▶ Deck of laminated child-size playing cards

▶ Junk mail envelopes

▶ Rubber stamp without ink

▶ Stuffed animals or dolls (pretend pals)

Setup

Use the scissors to cut a long, wide slit in the lid of the box for your child to drop each letter inside the mailbox. (Make this slit 10 inches long and ½ inch wide so that business-size envelopes can go in easily.)

Play for younger toddlers

Young toddlers should put each playing card in the slot of the shoebox mailbox. Spread the cards out on the floor, and supervise and help as needed to get all the cards inside the box. When all the cards are inside, take off the lid and let your child explore the cards, dump them out, and start all over again.

Play for older toddlers

Older toddlers can arrange the letters in piles, use the rubber stamp to "stamp" the letters with "ink," mail the letters, and even deliver the mail to parents, siblings, or the stuffed animals seated around the room.

39   **DRESS-UP**

AGE:
1–2 years

CATEGORY:
Solo Play/
Pretend

**NUMBER OF
CHILDREN:**
One

* SAFETY ALERT
Be sure to
remove any
small objects
(like buttons or
clips) that could
come loose and
pose a choking
hazard.

*Items like purses and wallets have a precious
grown-up quality for toddlers, who invent their
own special uses for them.*

Materials

▶ Plastic tub with lid (for storage)

▶ Hats: sailor hats, baseball caps, stocking caps,
straw hats

▶ Toddler-safe purses, wallets, backpacks, tote bags

▶ Child-size sunglasses (with lenses removed)

▶ Mittens or gloves

▶ Shoes*

▶ Adult-size vests*

Setup

Collect items at thrift stores and store them
in the "dress-up box" to keep your toddler
interested. An old baseball cap and vest may
transform your child into a busy construction
worker on a big job. A straw hat and gardening
gloves make for a farmer ready to tend to her
crops.

OFFICE

AGE:
1–2 years

CATEGORY:
Solo Play/
Pretend

**NUMBER OF
CHILDREN:**
One

NOTE
Starred
materials are
best for older
toddlers.

*If you work from home or if you've taken your
toddler along on a visit to the office, you know
that the concept of adult work is a source of
endless fascination and a subject for emulation.
A high chair can serve as an "office" space for
a younger toddler; older toddlers can be set up
at the kitchen table with their own special set
of office supplies. An old shoebox makes a good
"inbox."*

Materials

▸ Paper

▸ Crayons

▸ Junk mail envelopes

▸ Telephone

▸ Plastic wastebasket

▸ Shoebox

▸ Recycled book
(pages will get torn)*

▸ Index cards*

> **❝**
> Kids observe—they watch what you do, and their
> brain takes it in. And that becomes a model
> for how they're going to behave. Language
> is learned this way, and how to operate in the
> social world is learned that way too, so it's very,
> very important—this connection, this invisible
> brain-to-brain connection—in how kids learn and
> how they mature and grow up."
>
> **—Daniel Goleman, PhD**
> psychologist and author of
> *Emotional Intelligence* and *Social Intelligence*

TELEPHONE

AGE:
1–2 years

CATEGORY:
Solo Play/
Pretend

**NUMBER OF
CHILDREN:**
One

Telephone designs change with each passing year, but a toddler's fascination with this grown-up gadget never wanes. Give your older toddler a notepad and ask him to take a very important call from the office. Tell your younger child to call a relative or a friend.

Materials

▸ Toddler-safe toy telephone or toy cell phone

▸ Notepad and crayons, or toddler-safe office supplies (optional)

THE AMAZING PHONE

What a funny perception your toddler must have of the phone. He knows only what he sees with his own eyes or hears with his own ears, so he doesn't realize that you are actually talking to another person as you chat into the phone. Instead, your child simply sees a shiny object that vibrates or rings from time to time. When it rings, you stop what you are doing, pick it up, and talk and laugh into it. It's easy to see why a phone holds so much interest.

GROCERY STORE

AGE:
1–2 years

CATEGORY:
Solo Play/
Pretend

**NUMBER OF
CHILDREN:**
One

* SAFETY ALERT
Starred props
and toys are
intended for
older toddlers
who no longer
put objects in
their mouths.

Younger children may enjoy simply putting pretend groceries (containers) inside the shopping bag and dragging them from place to place, while an older child might want to emulate the entire food selection and preparation process (in that case, you might provide a wallet to encourage paying at the checkout line!).

Materials

▸ Cloth tote bag with handles (shopping bag)
▸ Juice boxes
▸ Cake mix or pudding boxes*
▸ Empty plastic milk jugs with handle (remove lids)*
▸ Cardboard egg carton*
▸ Empty plastic bottles (remove lids to prevent choking hazard)*
▸ Yogurt or margarine tubs
▸ Diaper wipe tubs
▸ Petroleum jelly containers
▸ Unbreakable peanut butter jars

Setup

Try a prompt like, "Do you want to go to your grocery store in the cupboard and buy some things for me to make for dinner tonight?" Your child's version of "grocery store" will be underway in no time.

STORY TIME/LIBRARY

AGE:
1–2 years

CATEGORY:
Solo Play/
Pretend

**NUMBER OF
CHILDREN:**
One

Books are nice to read, but they're great props for role-play too.

Materials

▶ Plastic bin full of board books

▶ Cloth tote bag

▶ Older children's or grown-up books
(ones you won't mind getting a little beat up)

▶ Stuffed animals and dolls
(the children for story-time reading)

Setup

Put together a bin of board books that your toddler can handle on her own. Turning pages, pointing to objects in the book, and emulating parents reading are all part of the fun. Older toddlers may "read" stories to a favorite teddy bear. Or perhaps they will become the children's librarian, reading stories to imaginary children gathered in a circle and later checking out books and slipping them inside a book bag.

44 | COOK

AGE:
1–2 years

CATEGORY:
Solo Play/
Pretend

**NUMBER OF
CHILDREN:**
One

Oh, the thrilling things that go on in a kitchen! The sounds (bacon frying in a pan, blenders whirling, dishes clinking), the smells, the sights, the action. . . . With an assortment of kitchen-related materials, the play will come naturally as your child imitates everything that's happening.

Materials

▶ Plastic measuring cups and spoons

▶ Unbreakable salt and pepper shakers (empty)

▶ Plastic or stainless steel mixing bowls

▶ Plastic cookie cutters (no small parts)

▶ Squeeze bottles

▶ Unbreakable muffin tins

▶ Child-size rolling pin

▶ Plastic cups and plates

▶ Plastic containers with lids

▶ Pie pan, cake pan, cooking pot, or cookie sheet

▶ Spatula and toddler-safe cooking utensils

Setup

Put the little chef on the floor or in a high chair. Then place a request! Favorite dishes are good options, but so are those with funny names—pineapple upside-down cake, for example.

RESTAURANT

AGE:
1–2 years

CATEGORY:
Solo Play/
Pretend

**NUMBER OF
CHILDREN:**
One

★ **SAFETY ALERT**
Starred
materials are
best for older
toddlers.

Restaurants are action-packed places. Waiters scurry around with big platters while sound effects abound!

Materials

▸ Unbreakable bowls, cups, and small spoons

▸ Empty juice boxes

▸ Food or pretend foods

▸ Plastic soda bottles (partially filled with water for pouring)*

▸ Notepad and crayon (for writing down orders)*

▸ Cloth napkins*

Setup

You'll need to set up the temporary restaurant for your child. Help him fold the napkins and show him how you set the table. Your younger toddler's restaurant play may end up looking more like the feast of a caveman than that of a four-star diner, but banging the bowls with a spoon and moving things from place to place are all part of the exploratory play experience. Older toddlers might get the hang of folding cloth napkins and pouring water as they "serve" their patrons.

TAKING CARE OF BABY

AGE:
1–2 years

CATEGORY:
Solo Play/
Pretend

**NUMBER OF
CHILDREN:**
One

Rocking a sweet, tiny plastic baby to sleep is a very responsible way of playing grown-up. And imaginary responsibilities are wonderful, because the possibilities are limitless—one minute your toddler could be putting baby down for a nap, and the next, they could be flying a plane together!

Materials

▸ Toddler-safe baby doll and baby bottle

▸ Shoebox (for baby bed)

▸ Baby blanket

▸ Plastic cup, bowl, and baby spoon

▸ Small plastic dishpan and sponge

▸ Board books

Setup

If your child seems to be establishing a regular nurturing routine with baby, you may want to set up the "bed" (shoebox) in a permanent place. The only time your older toddler might need assistance is if it becomes necessary to give baby a bath (hygiene is very important to toddlers too). Set him up with a dishpan with just a slight amount of water in it and a sponge (no soap).

FIXER-UPPER

AGE:
1–2 years

CATEGORY:
Solo Play/
Pretend

**NUMBER OF
CHILDREN:**
One

* SAFETY ALERT

Be sure
to provide
plastic tools
with rounded
ends and no
sharp edges
whatsoever.

*Tools are what separate us from other animals;
a toddler's first experience with tools is an
important developmental step. They're also the
ultimate mechanism for discovering how things
work—something toddlers love to do.*

Materials

▸ Plastic children's tools* (hammer, saw, wrench,
screwdriver, garden tools, etc.)

▸ Plastic toolbox or carrying case with a handle

▸ Objects that require "fixing"

▸ Ride-on toys

▸ Toy shopping cart, wagons, doll stroller,
toy lawn mower

▸ Kitchen chairs, kitchen table (legs can be "sawed"
and "tightened")

Play for younger toddlers

Young toddlers will enjoy hauling the tools
around from place to place in a toolbox
that they can open and close on their own.
Dumping the tools out and putting them
back in the box again is a big (temporarily
messy) part of the fun. They may do a bit of
enthusiastic banging and pounding with these
tools too, so get ready for a bit of noise.

Play for older toddlers

Older toddlers love to pretend to fix any toy
that has wheels. (This is particularly true
if your child has ever seen you fixing a car,

bike, or lawn mower.) They may also use their tools to repair the hinges and handles on low kitchen cupboards or other safe furniture around your home. A set of wooden blocks can easily be incorporated into fixer-upper play to fix or build things in your child's "shop" as well. Busy toddlers don't stay in one place very long, so it's likely that everything in sight will be "fixed" in very short order!

PEEKABOO WITH BOXES

Young toddlers love to play open-and-close and now-you-see-it-now-you-don't games with boxes. Your sixteen-month-old might drop a tennis ball inside a shoebox, put the lid on, and see that the ball has vanished from sight. When your child opens the lid, the ball is there once again. Toddlers repeat this routine again and again and again as they play, and fascinating discoveries are being made along the way. Your child begins to realize that just because an object can't be seen in the moment doesn't mean it is gone forever. This bit of wisdom later gets applied to other aspects of your toddler's life. For example, they will discover that important people (parents, grandparents, siblings, caregivers) vanish from sight for a while but reappear later. According to early childhood development specialists, a child is learning about object permanence when playing in this way.

2

PARENT & CHILD PLAY

Whenever I read a promo for an electronic toy that uses the word *interactive*, I have to chuckle. Interacting with a machine pales in comparison to interacting with a living, breathing human being. All the bells and whistles in the world can't change that.

Parents (and caregivers) are fabulous play partners for toddlers. A mom rolls a ball, and her nineteen-month-old son rolls it back with a squeal. A dad hops up and down and makes a monkey sound, and his thirty-month-old daughter joins in with a game of Follow the Leader. These interactions create a package deal that can't be beat. The toddler gets her parents' undivided attention, which she adores. And she learns new skills and builds up stamina and muscle power in the most playful, delightful way.

INDOOR PLAY

Setting aside time to play indoors together makes for fun times, but also sends the message early on that play can (and should) be a part of everyday life. Toddlers learn that home is a safe place to explore and navigate—where living and playing are indistinguishable.

CLAPPING AND COUNTING GAMES

When your child is not feeling well (or even if her mood is just a bit subdued), traditional clapping and counting games might be just the ticket to pass the time in a waiting room. The rhythms are comforting, and the finger play creates a bit of added interest to hold your child's attention.

Developmentally, your toddler will be able to hold her hands open, but she may not be able to clap on her own just yet. You can help her clap by holding her hands and gently clapping them together or by letting her hold on to your hands while you clap. The repetitive nature of the action and language of the rhymes will delight your toddler (who will ask you to repeat them again and again) and help develop her hand–eye coordination and language skills as she plays.

TWO LITTLE BLACKBIRDS

AGE:
1–2 years

CATEGORY:
Parent &
Child Play/
Indoor

**NUMBER OF
CHILDREN:**
One

Two little blackbirds
(*wiggle your two index fingers*)

Sitting on a hill,
(*wiggle two fingers again*)

One named Jack,
(*crook one finger*)

One named Jill.
(*crook the other finger*)

Fly away, Jack!
(*wiggle the "Jack" finger as you move it
behind your back*)

Fly away, Jill!
(*wiggle the "Jill" finger as you move it behind
your back*)

Come back, Jack,
(*bring the "Jack" finger back as you wiggle it*)

Come back, Jill,
(*bring the "Jill" finger back as you wiggle it*)

Two little blackbirds
(*wiggle both index fingers*)

Sitting on a hill.
(*wiggle both fingers again*)

(*REPEAT THE ENTIRE VERSE AND MOVEMENTS*)

49 PAT-A-CAKE

AGE:
1–2 years

CATEGORY:
Parent &
Child Play/
Indoor

**NUMBER OF
CHILDREN:**
One

Patty cake, patty cake, baker's man,
(*clap baby's hands together*)

Bake me a cake as fast as you can.
(*clap baby's hands together*)

Roll it and pat it and mark it with a *B*,
(*move baby's hands in a circle, clap them
together, and write an imaginary* B *on
baby's hands*)

And put it in the oven for baby and me!
(*put baby's hands together, move them
toward your mouth, and kiss or pretend
to nibble tops of baby's hand.*)

50 PITTY, PATTY, POLT

AGE:
1–2 years

CATEGORY:
Parent &
Child Play/
Indoor

**NUMBER OF
CHILDREN:**
One

Pitty, patty, polt,
(*tap on child's foot*)

Shoe a little colt,

Here a nail, there a nail,

Pitty, patty, polt.
(*tap on child's foot*)

51 PEAS PORRIDGE HOT

AGE:
1–2 years

CATEGORY:
Parent &
Child Play/
Indoor

**NUMBER OF
CHILDREN:**
One

Clap your hands while reciting this rhyme. Clap your hands on your legs. Clap your hands on your baby's knees. Or cross your hands to your chest between each clap. (Fill in the blanks with the name your child calls you.)

Peas porridge hot,

Peas porridge cold,

Peas porridge in the pot

Nine days old.

Some like it hot,

Some like it cold,

Some like it in the pot

Nine days old.

My _____ likes it hot,

My _____ likes it cold,

But I like it in the pot

Nine days old.

EENSY WEENSY SPIDER

AGE:
1–2 years

CATEGORY:
Parent &
Child Play/
Indoor

**NUMBER OF
CHILDREN:**
One

(Also called the "Itsy Bitsy Spider")

The eensy weensy spider

Went up the waterspout.
*(place tip of right thumb on left forefinger;
while these fingers are joined, swivel both
hands so that the left thumb joins up with
the right forefinger; release the bottom pair
of fingers and swivel them back to the top;
continue to alternate joining and releasing
each pair of fingers)*

Down came the rain

And washed the spider out!
*(hold your hands in the air and wiggle your
fingers to imitate rain)*

Out came the sun

And dried up all the rain.
*(hold your arms in the air in the shape of
a circle)*

So the eensy weensy spider

Went up the spout again.
*(create a brief climbing action with your
fingers and thumbs)*

53 HICKORY, DICKORY, DOCK

AGE:
1–2 years

CATEGORY:
Parent &
Child Play/
Indoor

**NUMBER OF
CHILDREN:**
One

Hickory, Dickory, Dock,

The mouse ran up the clock.
(*use two fingers to gently "walk" up
baby's arm*)

The clock struck one
(*kiss baby's head*)

And down he run.
(*use two fingers to gently walk down
baby's arm*)

Hickory, Dickory, Dock!
(*hug and kiss baby*)

54 HIGGLETY PIGGLETY

AGE:
1–2 years

CATEGORY:
Parent &
Child Play/
Indoor

**NUMBER OF
CHILDREN:**
One

Higglety Pigglety Pop!
(*clap hands*)

The dog has eaten the mop.

The pig's in a hurry,
(*roll arms with hands in fists*)

The cat's in a flurry,

Higglety Pigglety Pop!
(*clap hands*)

55 ONE POTATO, TWO POTATO

AGE:
1–2 years

CATEGORY:
Parent &
Child Play/
Indoor

**NUMBER OF
CHILDREN:**
One

Clap while reciting this rhyme, or make a fist and knock the tops of other player's fists on each count.

One potato, two potato,

Three potato, four;

Five potato, six potato,

Seven potato more.

(*REPEAT THE ENTIRE VERSE AND MOVEMENTS*)

56 ONE, TWO, THREE

AGE:
1–2 years

CATEGORY:
Parent &
Child Play/
Indoor

**NUMBER OF
CHILDREN:**
One

One, two, three,
(*tap on baby's knee*)

Tickle your knee,
(*tickle baby's knee*)

Four, five, six,
(*tap on baby's tummy*)

Pick up sticks.
(*tickle baby's tummy*)

Seven, eight, nine,
(*tap on baby's chin*)

You're all mine!
(*big hug!*)

RHYMING GAMES

Have some fun creating your own simple rhyming games. Incorporate your child's name or favorite toy or familiar family activities you experience together. Here are a few of my own rhymes and rhyming games to serve as a sample. To get started, just sit on the floor facing each other and use the simple props listed to create action as you play.

57 BUSY AS CAN BE!

AGE:
1–2 years

CATEGORY:
Parent & Child Play/
Indoor

NUMBER OF CHILDREN:
One

The kitchen is a busy, bustling little world to enjoy together.

Materials

▶ 2 spoons (1 for parent, 1 for child)

Rhyme

(*Substitute your child's name for "Lucy."*)

Working in the kitchen, Lucy and me,
(*point to child, then to self*)

Stirring, stirring, busy as can be,
(*stir around and around with the spoon*)

One spoon for Lucy, one spoon for me,
(*have a quick taste from the spoon*)

Working in the kitchen, happy as can be.

(*Invent more verses, using your child's favorite foods and kitchen gadgets.*)

DOGGIE, DOGGIE

AGE:
1–2 years

CATEGORY:
Parent &
Child Play/
Indoor

**NUMBER OF
CHILDREN:**
One

*A small beanbag masquerades as a
"doggie bone" in this game of lost and found.*

Materials

▶ Small toddler-safe beanbag (the bone)

▶ Toy telephone

▶ Unbreakable bowl

▶ Stuffed animal (preferably a dog)

Rhyme

*(Before you get started, tuck the beanbag
in your back pocket or waistband.)*

Doggie, Doggie, where's your bone?

Underneath the telephone?
(pick up the phone to look)

No sir, no sir, it's not there.
(shake your head no)

Tell me, tell me, tell me where.
(turn up both hands to show your palms)

Did the kitty take it and put it in her bowl?
(look inside bowl)

Did your mama hide it, deep down in a hole?
(look at ground, hands in lookout position)

Doggie, Doggie, where's your treat?
*(keeping the "bone" [beanbag] hidden
in your hand, slide it under Doggie's feet)*

I declare, it's at your feet!

THROUGH AND THROUGH!

AGE:
1–2 years

CATEGORY:
Parent &
Child Play/
Indoor

**NUMBER OF
CHILDREN:**
One

*Learn a rhyming song that teaches the senses,
the parts of the body, and unconditional love.*

Rhyme

(*Fill in the blanks with the name your child
calls you.*)

I'm your _____ through and through,

Let me take a look at you.
(*hands over eyes in lookout position,
looking from side to side*)

I see you with my eyes,
(*point to your eyes*)

Big as pumpkin pies.

I hear you with my ears,
(*pull out your ears*)

Hanging here for many years.
(*tug on your earlobes*)

I'm your _____ through and through,

Let me give a kiss to you!
(*kiss baby*)

(*Invent similar rhymes about a favorite
doll, teddy bear, or family pet!*)

SONGS AND LULLABIES

Singing is a lovely gift to give to your child and introduces music into your child's life in a natural and comforting way. It offers a dose of fun for both the singer and the listener. Here are some classic children's songs that may inspire you to recall musical memories from your own childhood. You'll have the opportunity to create charming stories too as you invent silly rhymes for your child's own version of "Hush Little Baby" (see Personal Lullaby variation, page 94). The joyful musical experiences that you share with your toddler will help make music a familiar and expected part of daily life. A splendid gift, indeed.

60 TWINKLE, TWINKLE

AGE:
1–2 years

CATEGORY:
Parent & Child Play/ Indoor

NUMBER OF CHILDREN:
One

Twinkle, twinkle little star,
How I wonder what you are!

Up above the world so high,
Like a diamond in the sky.

Twinkle, twinkle little star,
How I wonder what you are.

61 ARE YOU SLEEPING?

AGE:
1–2 years

CATEGORY:
Parent &
Child Play/
Indoor

**NUMBER OF
CHILDREN:**
One

English version ("Are You Sleeping?")

Are you sleeping,
Are you sleeping,
Brother John, Brother John?

Morning bells are ringing,
Morning bells are ringing.

Ding, ding, dong, ding, ding, dong.

French version ("Frère Jacques")

Frère Jacques, Frère Jacques,
Dormez-vous,
Dormez-vous?

Sonnez les matines,
Sonnez les matines.

Ding, deng, dong, ding, deng, dong.

It really troubles me when I see parents driving
to nursery school with kids watching TV in the
back of the SUV. That time is precious, when
driving the children—to sing songs, to play
games, to talk."

—David Elkind, PhD
professor emeritus of child development at Tufts University
and author of *The Hurried Child* and *The Power of Play*

PERSONAL LULLABY

AGE:
1–2 years

CATEGORY:
Parent &
Child Play/
Indoor

**NUMBER OF
CHILDREN:**
One

*Use favorite family words to invent your own
special verses for classic lullabies (fill in the
blanks with the name your child calls you). Here
is a sample from my friend Kiki Walker:*

Hush little baby, don't you cry,
_____'s gonna find you a butterfly,

And if that butterfly won't light,
_____'s gonna buy you a big red kite.

And if that big red kite does break,
_____'s gonna make you a chocolate cake.

And if that chocolate cake won't keep,
_____'s gonna sing you fast asleep!

66

Parents should sing to their children, and they
should sing like they mean it, like they love
these songs. Most children, if they're given the
opportunity, are going to love playing games,
singing songs, and dancing around the living
room with music—especially if a parent is doing
it as well."

—John Feierabend, PhD
professor emeritus of music education
at the Hartt School at the University of Hartford,
and author of the First Steps in Music series

BAA, BAA, BLACK SHEEP

AGE:
1–2 years

CATEGORY:
Parent &
Child Play/
Indoor

**NUMBER OF
CHILDREN:**
One

Baa, baa, black sheep,
Have you any wool?
Yes sir, yes sir,
Three bags full.

One for the master,
One for the dame,
And one for the little boy
Who lives down the lane.

Baa, baa, black sheep,
Have you any wool?
Yes sir, yes sir,
Three bags full.

READING ALOUD

Reading aloud is a beautiful way for grown-ups and toddlers to play. Think of books as toys; you are a special playmate who can make these toys come alive for your child. You open the book to a page with colorful pictures and you begin to read aloud. As you do so, you activate your child's sense of hearing, sight, and touch as you explore the book.

But the magic doesn't stop there. Your child is getting comfortable seeing letters and words in print and turning pages of the book. These early experiences set the stage for learning letters, recognizing words, and eventually learning to read. Reading picture books together during the toddler years is truly a very important way for your child to grow through play! You'll discover your own favorites, but here are some of my picks to add to your list. Keep in mind that the age classification system for books is flexible. Your one-year-old may still enjoy the books you read when he was an infant.

RECOMMENDED READING

Are You My Mother?
by P. D. Eastman

Barnyard Dance!
by Sandra Boynton

**Big Dog and
Little Dog series**
by Dav Pilkey

**Brown Bear, Brown
Bear, What Do You See?**
by Bill Martin Jr.,
illustrations by Eric
Carle

Each Peach Pear Plum
by Janet Ahlberg and
Allan Ahlberg

The Everything Book
by Denise Fleming

Freight Train
by Donald Crews

Goodnight Moon
by Margaret Wise
Brown, illustrations
by Clement Hurd

**Guess How Much
I Love You**
by Sam McBratney,
illustrations by
Anita Jeram

**Have You Seen
My Duckling?**
by Nancy Tafuri

I Can
by Helen Oxenbury

The Itsy-Bitsy Spider
by Rosemary Wells

I Went Walking
by Sue Williams,
illustrations by
Julie Vivas

Max's First Word
by Rosemary Wells

Maybe My Baby
by Irene O'Book,
photos by
Paula Hible

Moo Baa La La La
by Sandra Boynton

**My Very First
Mother Goose**
by Iona Opie,
illustrations by
Rosemary Wells

**Old Macdonald
Had a Farm**
by Pam Adams

Owl Babies
by Martin Waddell,
illustrations by
Patrick Benson

Pat the Bunny
by Dorothy Kunhardt

The Runaway Bunny by Margaret Wise Brown, illustrations by Clement Hurd

Sheep in a Jeep by Nancy Shaw, illustrations by Margot Apple

Silly Little Goose! by Nancy Tafuri

Sleep Tight, Little Bear by Martin Waddell, illustrations by Barbara Firth

The Snowy Day by Ezra Jack Keats

The Teddy Bears' Picnic by Jimmy Kennedy, illustrations by Alexandra Day

Three Little Kittens by Paul Galdone

Toes, Ears, & Nose! by Marion Dane Bauer, illustrations by Karen Katz

Welcome, Baby! Baby Rhymes for Baby Times by Stephanie Calmenson, illustrations by Melissa Sweet

Whose Mouse Are You? by Robert Kraus and Jose Aruego

When you're playing with a toddler with a book, the important thing is the interaction between the parent and the child. So if your toddler is more interested in pointing to the pictures and naming them, or making the animal sounds, or flipping the pages, then that's what you should be doing."

—Betty Bardige, PhD
developmental psychologist and coauthor of
Poems to Learn to Read By

ACTION GAMES

Toddlers love to show you what they know and what they can do. And with movement and fun blended together, the excitement is contagious.

64 | MONEY SEARCH

AGE:
2 years

CATEGORY:
Parent &
Child Play/
Indoor

**NUMBER OF
CHILDREN:**
One

The exhange of money often mesmerizes toddlers. Here, toddlers collect their own dollars and put them inside their very own wallet.

Materials

▸ Pretend (paper) money (available at toy stores)
▸ Invisible tape
▸ Oversize blank playing cards (available at teacher supply stores) or large index cards
▸ Scissors (for adult use only)
▸ Wallet from the dress-up bin

Setup

Tape one toy dollar to a blank playing card or index card and trim the excess card and dollar. "Hide" these dollars around the room, leaving half of each dollar in plain sight.

Play

Give your child the wallet to hold. Find the first dollar together and encourage your child to put it away in the wallet. Walk around the room with your child and nudge him in the right direction (if needed) to find all the remaining hidden dollars.

65 FIND THE BEANBAG!

AGE:
1–2 years

CATEGORY:
Parent &
Child Play/
Indoor

**NUMBER OF
CHILDREN:**
One

* SAFETY ALERT
Discard or repair
any beanbags
with tears, which
can present a
choking hazard.

*There is a young detective lurking in every
toddler, and this type of game brings it right out.*

Materials

▸ Toddler-safe beanbag*
(available at teacher supply stores)

▸ 4 or more quart-size plastic tubs
(ice cream or yogurt containers, for example)

Setup

Place the tubs upside down on the floor in
a straight line. Have your toddler close her
eyes (or wait until her attention wanders for
a moment) and slip the beanbag under one
of the tubs.

Play

Tell your child that you've hidden a beanbag
under one of the tubs. Now it's time to "find
the beanbag!" Encourage her to turn over each
tub until she finds it. After you've played for
a few minutes in this way, your older toddler
may enjoy hiding the beanbag and turning
the tables. In this case, cover your eyes during
the hiding phase. When she's done hiding she
calls out, "Find the beanbag!"

66 FIND THE ANIMAL!

Shoeboxes are terrific for hide-and-seek object
play—toddlers love taking the lids off and
on and looking inside. You can play a similar

game using shoeboxes and a small stuffed animal. Or, as your child nears three years old, you could vary the game by adding an element of color identification. Use red, yellow, green, and blue beanbags and ask your toddler to find a specific color.

67 BEANBAG TOSS

AGE:
2 years

CATEGORY:
Parent &
Child Play/
Indoor

**NUMBER OF
CHILDREN:**
One

Beanbags have a good feel and are easy for small hands to hold, so they are a good choice for early tossing games.

Materials

▸ Dishpan

▸ Toddler-safe beanbags*
(available at teacher supply stores)

* SAFETY ALERT

Discard or repair any beanbags with tears, which can present a choking hazard.

Setup

Place the dishpan in the center of the room with the beanbags on the floor nearby.

Play

Toss one beanbag inside the dishpan to give your toddler the idea of how to play. Younger toddlers won't need much distance to enjoy this game. Older toddlers can stand a foot or two away to toss the beanbags inside the dishpan.

68 TEDDY SAYS . . .

AGE:
1–2 years

CATEGORY:
Parent &
Child Play/
Indoor

**NUMBER OF
CHILDREN:**
One

It's a variation on the classic "Where are your ears, your eyes, your nose?" with a touch of Simon Says thrown in for good measure!

Materials

▶ Favorite teddy bear or stuffed animal

Play for younger toddlers

Young toddlers will learn to point to their head, eyes, nose, ears, elbows, feet, etc. Bring in the furry third party by starting each request with "Teddy" ("Teddy says touch your eyes," "Teddy says show me your nose"). As toddlers become a bit older, they will understand many more words and be capable of more physical movements. Extend this game to more complex physical actions by saying, "Teddy says jump up and down," or "Teddy says turn around."

Play for older toddlers

Your older toddler can play a more elaborate version of Teddy Says. To start the game, prop up the stuffed animal and announce that Teddy wants to see some of the things that your child has learned to do for herself. Create a series of requests: "Teddy says rub your tummy"; "Teddy says pat your head"; "Teddy says touch the ground." Let your child's understanding of language and her physical abilities lead the way as to which commands from Teddy are included in the game. Add some silly requests to make this game lively and fun. Once your child is familiar with the game, let her become the voice of Teddy and take a turn making Teddy requests that you must perform: "Teddy says hop"; "Teddy says touch your mouth"; etc.

There are a lot of scientific principles involved in some of the simpler activities of early childhood. We have to actually have experiences to understand cause and effect, and we have to have experiences in order to understand a sequence of things. . . . We have to have experiences of touching and feeling and manipulating to get the concepts of bigger and smaller, more and less—all the concepts that will later be important in mathematics, in science, in reading. As adults we take those things for granted, but those are really complex understandings for a little child."

—Jane M. Healy, PhD
educational psychologist and author of
Your Child's Growing Mind and *Failure to Connect:
How Computers Affect Our Children's Minds*

69 | COLOR POCKETS

AGE:
2 years

CATEGORY:
Parent &
Child Play/
Indoor

**NUMBER OF
CHILDREN:**
One

*A color matching game for older toddlers who are
starting to recognize colors.*

Materials

▸ Library pockets (available at teacher supply stores)
▸ Foam board or cardboard (20 inches by 30 inches)
▸ Invisible tape
▸ Scissors (for adult use only)
▸ Construction paper (green, blue, yellow, red, white,
orange)
▸ Glue stick
▸ Small bucket or bowl

Setup

Arrange the library pockets in two rows on
the foam board and tape them firmly in place.
Cut a square of each color construction paper
(green, blue, yellow, red, white, and orange)
and glue one color to each of the pockets.
(Toddlers love to use glue sticks—with
supervision, of course—so if there's time,
let your toddler help with the gluing.) Next,
cut squares from the remaining construction
paper to match each of the six colors on the
library pockets. Fold these squares in half or
quarters for easier handling for your toddler
and place all the color squares in the bucket
and mix them around.

Play

Your child pulls a colored paper square from the bucket and tucks it inside the library pocket of the same color, continuing the matching process until all the colors have been used. (You may need to give a little assistance to get the paper squares out of each pocket once the game is over.) As your child gets older and knows more colors, add more library pockets with new and different colors to the foam board to expand this game.

COLOR DOT HIDE-AND-SEEK

AGE:
2 years

CATEGORY:
Parent &
Child Play/
Indoor

**NUMBER OF
CHILDREN:**
One

Color recognition is an exciting phase in a child's development. Suddenly, the world comes alive with red fire trucks, bright green apples, blue skies. . . . Here's a game that celebrates your toddler's first stabs at color sorting.

Materials

▸ Sheets of peel-off color dot stickers (available at office supply stores)
▸ Pack of index cards or blank make-your-own flash cards (available at teacher supply stores)
▸ Paper lunch bags
▸ Invisible tape

Setup

Select two or more colors that your child recognizes, say red and yellow. Peel and stick one yellow dot in the center of six blank cards. Peel and stick one red dot on six additional blank flash cards. Open two paper lunch bags and tape one of the yellow-dot cards on the outside of one bag and a red-dot card on the other bag. Place the two bags on the floor.

Play

Have your child sit on a chair or on the floor while you hide the cards faceup, in very visible places around the room. Now give your child the yellow-dot bag and ask her to find all the cards with yellow circles and put them inside. Once all these cards have been found, give your child the red-dot bag and have her do the same with the red-dot cards. Expand this game with more colors, or add cards with shapes, numbers, or alphabet letters when your child gets a bit older.

NONTOXIC ART SUPPLIES

Seek them out! You'll find a wide assortment of nontoxic art supplies—finger paints, watercolors, washable paints, chalk, crayons, glue, ink pads, and more—at your local school or teacher supply store. Look for the nontoxic symbol on these products: AP (Approved Product seal) surrounded by the words "ACMI Arts & Creative Materials Institute Certified."

ARTS AND CRAFTS

Toddlers are enthusiastic artists. What fun to have a crayon and paper when you are fourteen months old and making your creative mark for the very first time! Making art as a young toddler is all about experimentation—and the joy of messing around with art materials is no small prize.

Though art making does not necessarily entail collaborative play, I have included Arts and Crafts for toddlers in the Parent & Child Play section of this book because grown-up setup, supervision, and cleanup are required. Having said this, you'll find a mix of messy play ideas (best to try when you're both in good moods!) and no-fuss (no-mess) ideas like scribbling on paper. Knowing that parents sometimes like to get creative too, at the end of this section I've included a few craft projects that the two of you can do together. Some toddlers love seeing the end product that they've created, others are more enthralled with the process. Either way, there's good stuff going on as you scribble, paint, paste, and glue together.

STICKY PAPER

AGE:
1–2 years

CATEGORY:
Parent &
Child Play/
Indoor

**NUMBER OF
CHILDREN:**
One

Here's another activity that celebrates the joy of smearing glue on paper.

Materials

▸ Colored construction paper

▸ Large (nontoxic) glue stick

▸ Masking tape or painter's tape

▸ Large cookie sheet

Setup

Place a stack of construction paper on the table along with the glue stick. Tape a sheet of paper to the cookie sheet. (This holds the paper in place for vigorous gluing and contains the mess.)

Play

Offer a little demo to get things moving for the youngest toddlers. First, use the glue stick to smear some glue on the paper stuck to the cookie sheet. Add a clean sheet of paper and use your hand to rub the top sheet of paper so the pages stick together. Let your toddler use the glue stick to apply glue to the new top sheet of paper and continue to add more layers of paper to the paper-sandwich. The finished product is simply a stack of colored papers, but the joyful process of learning to glue is worth the mess. (For cleanup, remove the paper and tape from the cookie sheet and wash it to remove all the glue.)

SCRIBBLE LUNCH BAGS

AGE:
1–2 years

CATEGORY:
Parent &
Child Play/
Indoor

**NUMBER OF
CHILDREN:**
One

Toddlers like to scribble on flattened lunch bags; there's great fun in turning an everyday object into a piece of art. Post-transformation, the flattened bag can be opened up and used as a receptacle for all sorts of things.

Materials

▸ Paper lunch bags

▸ Crayons

Setup

Place a stack of flattened paper lunch bags and an assortment of chunky crayons on the table.

Play

Select a crayon to begin making your own drawing, or scribble, on a bag, and your toddler will soon follow suit. Once you've finished coloring a few bags, set them aside to save for lunch, or open one or more bags and stand them up in the middle of the table. Then put a few items inside (a flower, a cookie, or a small stuffed animal), and fold a 2-inch or 3-inch flap down to make it easy to carry the bag. Some toddlers will continue coloring and some will redirect their attention to their new colorful accessory. If your toddler gets going and starts to produce in any quantity, you might want to decorate a shoebox to hold all the fancy lunch bags.

73 FANCY-SHMANCY COOKIE PLATES

If you're baking cookies (and the excitement is building), your little artist can create special cookie-serving plates with colorful drawings and designs. Use thin paper plates and crayons.

SCRIBBLE BOOKMARKS

AGE:
1–2 years

CATEGORY:
Parent &
Child Play/
Indoor

**NUMBER OF
CHILDREN:**
One

*Toddler art isn't just for hanging on the wall!
These easy-to-make bookmarks are perfect
homemade gifts for Grandma, Grandpa, and
other extended family members, and since
the surface area is small, they might be less
intimidating to a toddler than a full piece of
paper.*

Materials

▸ Recycled vinyl or cloth tablecloth
  (that you don't mind getting scribbles on)

▸ Invisible tape

▸ Pack of blank make-your-own flash cards
  (available at teacher supply stores)

▸ Nontoxic, washable markers

Setup

Put the tablecloth on the floor or kitchen table
as a protective layer for toddler scribbling
and drawing. Put the art supplies on the work
area. Use invisible tape to tape one of the flash
cards to the table so it stays in place while
your child decorates and draws on it. Tape
another card in place for you to draw on. Start
drawing on your own flash card and provide
markers for your toddler to scribble on his.
Use a marker to write your child's name and
the date the drawing was created on the back
of each bookmark. Collect these bookmarks in
a shoebox or special envelope and send them
out to loved ones on birthdays and holidays.

ODE TO DRAWING

Scribbling and drawing are simple, natural, self-directed ways for toddlers to experience the joy of making art. Toddlers will draw in their own way, sometimes with tentative marks, other times in robust scribbles that cover the page. Just show your child how to get started and let him enjoy the process. This "anything goes" approach, which doesn't focus on the results, sets the stage for creative self-expression that blossoms at each stage of childhood. And the humble action of drawing on paper is powerful: Learning to hold and manipulate crayons is a wonderful way to develop the fine motor skills needed to write letters and numbers in the next couple of years. An early familiarity with making (and seeing) letters and words on paper promotes a love of reading too. Your job is simply to provide some chunky crayons (or nontoxic markers), assorted paper (tape it to the table to help the youngest ones), and stand aside to let the magic begin. And be forewarned, toddlers will just as happily draw on the table, floors, and walls, as they will on paper!

SAFETY ALERT: Always supervise carefully to keep kids safe with crayons and markers.

TORN PAPER COLLAGE

AGE:
1–2 years

CATEGORY:
Parent &
Child Play/
Indoor

**NUMBER OF
CHILDREN:**
One or more

* SAFETY ALERT

Please supervise
your child so
that neither
the glue nor
the ziplock bag
creates a safety
hazard.

*This is a swanky name for an activity that lets
toddlers tear paper (which they love to do) and
mess around with glue (which they also love to do)!*

Materials

▸ Old bedsheet or newspapers

▸ Nontoxic white glue* (or homemade glue-paste,
see box on page 115)

▸ Small plastic mug or spill-proof paint pot

▸ Paintbrush

▸ Washcloth

▸ Ziplock bag*

▸ Colored construction paper

▸ Colored tissue paper or small pieces of
wrapping paper

Setup

Spread the old bedsheet or newspapers on
the kitchen table (for easy cleanup). Pour
a small amount of glue into the spill-proof
container or mug, and add just enough water
to thin the glue so it's easily spreadable with
a paintbrush. Wet the washcloth and place it
inside the ziplock bag. Put it on the table to use
as a wipe when hands get sticky.

Play

You and your child each get a few pieces
of construction paper, tissue paper, and/or
wrapping paper, and begin tearing various
size pieces. When you've gathered a pile of
colorful shreds of paper, begin assembling

your Torn Paper Collage on a fresh piece of construction paper. Use the paintbrush to dab little bits of glue on the construction paper and select pieces of torn paper to lay on top of the glue. Continue working together (or each on your own separate sheets of paper) to glue lots of shreds of paper on the page to form a multicolor collage. (Some parents find that their child loves to specialize in slopping glue on the page while the grown-up adds scraps of paper. Use whatever teamwork plan seems best for you.)

HOMEMADE GLUE-PASTE FOR TODDLERS

Whether you're in a pinch or you're looking for a way to make sure your glue is 100 percent nontoxic, you can whip up this easy glue-paste from flour and water. It won't have exactly the same "sticking" properties as store-bought glue, but it's a good bet for toddlers, who enjoy the process of gluing. Here's how to make it:

⅓ cup all-purpose unbleached white flour

2 tablespoons sugar

1 cup water

Mix the flour and sugar together in a small pan. Pour the water in slowly, stirring and mixing as you pour. Cook over low heat for a few minutes, continuing to stir. Allow to cool thoroughly before your child uses for gluing.

76 | DIY ART BOX

PARENT TIP

"I bought a sturdy cardboard file box with handles from the office supply store and turned it into a toddler art supply box so all our art stuff is in one place. I gave my daughter, Lucy, sheets of yellow poster board to draw on. Then I cut these drawings to fit the sides and lid of the file box, used clear packaging tape to stick them on, and now her art supply box is decorated beautifully."

—Julia from Michigan

"

When children take their first physical steps, parents get so excited. But at exactly that same time, children make their first marks on paper, which is the beginning of drawing, writing, and reading, and all forms of literacy. So, parents need to be thinking not only 'Oh, my child's a year old—he or she is probably going to walk soon,' but 'My child's a year old, and my child's going to draw soon—I have to get crayons and paper and make sure that I make that a positive experience.'"

—Susan Striker
founder of Young at Art and author of
The Anti-Coloring Book series

PAINTING

AGE:
1–2 years

CATEGORY:
Parent &
Child Play/
Indoor

**NUMBER OF
CHILDREN:**
One or more

NOTE
To make
things easier,
designate one
color of paint
for beginning
painters and
provide one
spill-proof pot
of paint and one
brush! ("Today's
color is RED!")
As your child
gets used to
painting, you
can incorporate
more colors.

*Are you having a good day today? Then there's no
time like the present to introduce your toddler to
painting for the very first time!*

Materials

▸ Newsprint paper or butcher paper

▸ Nontoxic, washable paints

▸ Spill-proof paint pots

▸ Artist's or painter's brushes with short,
  stubby handles

▸ Large adult-size T-shirt or dress shirt
  (to use as a painter's smock)

Setup

Clip paper to an easel or set up a painting
area at a plastic play table. (See box on page
119 for paper setup and easy cleanup ideas.)
Dress your child in the smock and pour a
little paint in a paint pot and add one brush.

Play

There really are no rules and no "how-to"
about it, just let your child dip his brush
in the paint and start putting paint on the
paper. (Younger toddlers may prefer dabbing
to making brushstrokes.) Don't expect to
see pictures or representational artwork.
This is all about learning to handle paint
and brushes and having a bit of fun.

78 | PAINT DABBER

AGE:
2 years

CATEGORY:
Parent &
Child Play/
Indoor

**NUMBER OF
CHILDREN:**
One

*In little dibs and dabs, your toddler applies paint
to paper using a painter's sponge (on a stick).
This art play is a cross between painting and
printmaking.*

Materials

▸ Newspapers or old tablecloth
(to cover kitchen table)

▸ Nontoxic, washable paint

▸ Plastic picnic plates or disposable pie pan
(for paint palette)

▸ Newsprint paper or construction paper

▸ Small painter's sponge (with a wooden or
plastic handle to hold)

▸ Large adult-size T-shirt or dress shirt
(to use as a painter's smock)

Setup

Spread newspapers or an old tablecloth on
the kitchen table to ensure an easy cleanup.
Pour a little of one color of paint onto a plastic
plate. Place a large sheet of newsprint or
construction paper on the table and dress
your child in the smock.

Play

Help your toddler dab the sponge into the
paint for the first time (apply a little pressure
to saturate the sponge). Then move the sponge
to the paper and dab paint on the page. Let
your child experiment with repeated dabs all
over the paper from that first dollop of paint.

When the sponge gets dry, your child dips it into the paint again and continues to make dabs all over the page. After a while, you may want to pour another color of paint in a second plastic plate to add a second color to the painting. Rinse out the sponge and dip it into this second color.

A SPECIAL PAINTING PLACE

Painting is a fun but messy business for toddlers, so designate a special area and setup for toddler painting that includes a system for easy cleanup. A plastic or wooden preschool easel with a trough to hold a spill-proof container of paint is one way to ease cleanup woes. Since the process of dipping brushes in paint is what's most exciting to your child, limit your setup to one pot of paint. That one pot will provide loads of fun and will make cleanup easier too. Clips at the top of the easel hold large sheets of paper in place, but use tape along the sides to secure the paper more firmly to the easel. Another idea is to use a small, sturdy, toddler-size plastic table or picnic table for artwork: Tape butcher paper together to cover the entire table (creating one giant painting surface), and use tape to secure the paper to the table too. And always spread out a painter's drop cloth or old vinyl tablecloth underneath your little artiste's painting area!

ROLLER-PAINTING

AGE:
2 years

CATEGORY:
Parent &
Child Play/
Indoor

**NUMBER OF
CHILDREN:**
One or more

Grab your beret (or better yet, a shower cap), and let the good times roll! As anyone who's dabbled in house painting knows, a paint roller is good, squishy fun. Since this activity requires some dexterity, it's best for older toddlers.

Materials

▸ Roll of butcher paper (or large sheets of drawing paper or newsprint)

▸ Painter's tape or invisible tape

▸ Nontoxic, washable paint

▸ Disposable pie pan or plastic picnic plate

▸ Mini paint roller for interior house painting (available at hardware stores)

▸ Large adult-size T-shirt or dress shirt (to use as a painter's smock)

Setup

Cover a plastic play table (or outdoor picnic table) with butcher paper. Use tape to secure the paper to the table. Pour a small quantity of paint in the pan and dress your child in a smock.

Play

Dip the roller in the paint pan and let your child roll it back and forth across the paper. (Be ready to descend with the cleanup supplies as soon as it appears your child has taken his last stroke across the paper!)

SOCK PUPPET

AGE:
1–2 years

CATEGORY:
Parent &
Child Play/
Indoor

**NUMBER OF
CHILDREN:**
One

If an elaborate craft proves a test for your motor skills (or patience and time), here's a very simple activity even the least crafty parent can put together. All you need is a sock and a marker!

Materials

▸ White tube socks

▸ Nontoxic, washable markers

Setup

Simply slide a tube sock over your child's hand and arm and have him place his thumb opposite his other fingers inside the tip of the sock. As he opens and closes this grip, help form a big mouth at the end of the sock. Take notice of approximately where the eyes and face should be while the sock is on your child's hand.

Play

Take the sock off your toddler's hand, and use the washable markers to let him draw the eyes and mouth in the appropriate location on the sock.

81 ADVANCED SOCK PUPPET

For a more elaborate puppet (and more parent involvement), the parent uses scissors to cut circles from felt and sews them on the sock. Draw eyebrows and a mouth with the washable markers for a complete face. Sew on strands of yarn so that they fall down along both sides of the face to create hair.

82 PUPPET ON A STICK

AGE:
2 years

CATEGORY:
Parent &
Child Play/
Indoor

**NUMBER OF
CHILDREN:**
One

If a craft session is called for and your art cupboard is bare, a paper plate, crayons, and scraps of fabric can save the day!

Materials

▸ Paper plates (regular size or small dessert plates)
▸ Clear, wide packaging tape or wide masking tape
▸ Wooden paint stir sticks or giant wooden craft sticks
▸ Nontoxic, washable markers
▸ Crayons
▸ Glitter glue or white liquid glue
▸ Scraps of yarn, ribbon, fabric

Setup

Turn the plate over (with eating side facedown) and securely tape the wooden stick to the back of the plate with several strips of tape. (The wooden stick becomes the handle, so make certain it is positioned so your child can easily hold it.)

Play

Help your child get started drawing a face on the front side of the plate using markers and crayons. Add glitter glue, and scraps of yarn, ribbon, or fabric for the hair, beard, or mustache.

83 PAPER PLATE MITTEN PUPPET

Place two sturdy paper plates together, so that the undersides of the plates are facing outward. Use masking tape to attach the outside edges. (Leave a space about 4 inches across the bottom of the plates unsecured, so that a child's hand can slip inside this mitten-style puppet.) Help your child decorate one side of the plate with a face and the other side with a different face so that your child has two pretend characters.

84 ANIMAL PHOTO PUPPETS

Clip color photos of animals or of people's faces from magazines. Help your toddler glue these photos to the paper plate, and use yarn for hair, a beard, or a mustache. Add a wooden stick for a handle, or make the mitten-style puppet above.

OUTDOOR PLAY

When you go outside to play, you've put your stamp of approval on the great outdoors, where the stimulus is abundant. Leaves don't need batteries to sway in the wind; birds don't need remote controls to fly. And best of all, they're free! Take your toddler outside, and any game you play comes alive to all the unexpected possibilities of the great outdoors.

85 | ROLL IT, TOSS IT

AGE:
1–2 years

CATEGORY:
Parent & Child Play/ Outdoor

NUMBER OF CHILDREN:
One

Is there a game more timeless than catch? This toddler version of catch is a warm-up that uses rolling or tossing to instill the concept.

Materials

▶ Beach ball (slightly deflated for better handling by the youngest toddlers)

Play

Younger toddlers will enjoy a simple game of rolling or throwing the ball back and forth with you; some nudging and demonstrating may be needed in order to get the game going. Older toddlers (with more advanced motor skills and language comprehension) will enjoy a game similar to Simon Says, where you call out "roll it" or "toss it" and your child follows along.

86 RINGER-BALL

AGE:
2 years

CATEGORY:
Parent &
Child Play/
Outdoor

**NUMBER OF
CHILDREN:**
One

Stand a Hula-Hoop upright to create a toddler-friendly tossing target. (And while you're at it, a quick hula demonstration never hurt anyone!)

Materials
▸ Newspaper (or foam balls, tennis balls, or beanbags)
▸ Large Hula-Hoop

Setup
Crumple up sheets of newspaper to make a pile of newspaper balls for tossing.

Play
Standing, hold the Hula-Hoop alongside your leg (about a foot off the ground) while your child tosses balls through the hoop from a short distance away.

87 RING-A-DING-SOCCER
Once your older toddler has mastered the art of elementary Ringer-Ball, you might introduce a soccer ball or similar and have him try to kick it through the Hula-Hoop (this time, hold it so it's resting on the ground).

TODDLER BASKETBALL

AGE:
1–2 years

CATEGORY:
Parent &
Child Play/
Outdoor

**NUMBER OF
CHILDREN:**
One

This game requires a little help from a grown-up basket-tender (holder) in the beginning, but older toddlers will squeal with delight when they get a "basket" on their own.

Materials

▸ Plastic tub (or small laundry basket)
▸ Soft, medium-size ball (easy for your child to grab and handle)

Play

Hold the basket at toddler height and have her throw or toss the ball into the basket. Don't forget that part of your job as basket tender is moving the basket to help catch the ball! As more skills and interests in ball games develop, vary the game a bit by having your toddler bounce the ball on the ground while you move in with the basket to catch the ball on the bounce.

Parents are more important to their child than any program or any other thing is, particularly in early childhood. So that time spent with them, reading, playing, talking, singing–that's the most valuable experience they can give their children."

—David Elkind, PhD
professor emeritus of child development at Tufts University
and author of *The Hurried Child* and *The Power of Play*

BOUNCY BALL

AGE:
1–2 years

CATEGORY:
Parent &
Child Play/
Outdoor

**NUMBER OF
CHILDREN:**
One

A bouncing ball is an endless source of fascination for a toddler. Here's a game that relies on simple teamwork between child and grown-up to bounce and catch the ball with a dishpan.

Materials

▶ Small bouncy ball

▶ Large plastic colander or dishpan with handles

Setup

Get your toddler excited about this game with a simple solo demonstration to set the stage for play. Hold the colander in one hand and bounce the ball on the ground. Quickly grab the colander with two hands and position it to catch the ball off the bounce.

Play

Your child uses two hands to bounce the ball (as hard as she can) on the ground, and you catch the ball off the bounce using the colander. As your toddler gains more bouncing skill and power behind each bounce, you can stand a fair distance away and run to scoop the ball with drama, flair, and sound effects!

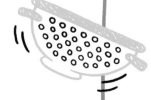

ZOOM, ZOOM, ZOOM!

AGE:
1–2 years

CATEGORY:
Parent &
Child Play/
Outdoor

**NUMBER OF
CHILDREN:**
One

*No, it's not a car commercial! This feisty game
has a name that is fun to say over and over again.*

Materials

▸ 6 or more tennis balls

▸ Small bucket with handles

▸ Plastic slide (with rounded edges for safety)

Setup

Place all the balls in the bucket.

Play

Stand on one side of the slide, holding the
bucket of balls; have your toddler stand
on the other side near the sliding board's
midpoint. Hand your child one ball at a time
and encourage her to release the ball onto
the slide and watch it zoom down onto the
lawn or playground. When all the balls have
zoomed down the slide, your child plays
"pick up" and puts all the balls back in the
bucket. Most young toddlers love this game
and will want to play again and again.

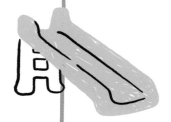

91 ZOOM UP

Families with a big-kid slide in the backyard or access to a big-kid slide can play this rolling game uphill. Stand at the very end of the slide and roll the tennis ball up the slide with a hearty thrust to see how far up it will go before it rolls right back down to your feet. Have your toddler join you in this riotous physics experiment. To add a bit of a challenge, position a small basket at the top end of the slide for a game of Zoom Up basketball. (Place a towel inside the basket to prevent erratic bounces.)

""

For children with cerebral palsy who have problems opening and closing their hands quickly enough to catch a ball, take an oven mitt and put a couple of rough pieces of Velcro on it. Then attach the opposite (soft) pieces of Velcro to a lightweight child-size ball. Toss that ball to the child while she's wearing the mitt that has the Velcro on it. And, as long as the ball touches the Velcro, she's going to catch the ball. It's a good game for children between eighteen months and up."

—Kristi Menear, PhD
professor of human studies
at the University of Alabama at Birmingham

92   FOLLOW THE LEADER

AGE:
2 years

CATEGORY:
Parent &
Child Play/
Outdoor

**NUMBER OF
CHILDREN:**
One

CLASSIC ACTIVITY

Toddlers love seeing a grown-up act silly in this classic game!

Setup

Think of all the physical skills (including making sounds) that your child has mastered before you start this game. Examples might include walking with hands in the air, hopping, clapping, galloping, barking like a dog, meowing like a cat, running to the fence, touching it, and running back again, etc.

Play

Play the part of the leader and make up a series of movements and sounds for your child to imitate.

93   ONE-TWO-THREE, HOP LIKE ME

Make up your own counting rhyme and add some actions to match:

One, two, three . . . hop like me.
(*hop, hop, hop*)

Four, five, six . . . pick up sticks.
(*bend down, pretend to pick up sticks,
and pop back up again*)

Seven, eight, nine . . . do the monkeyshine.
(*somersault, roll around, etc.*)

And then there's ten . . . cluck like a hen.
(*invent a funny "chicken walk" and add
sound effects*)

ANATOMY OF A MUD PUDDLE

Sure, mud is messy and a kid's muddy play clothes do need to be washed, but mud puddles are so much fun! A quick look at a puddle's properties gives a hint as to why little kids like to mess around in them. First, there's the thrilling surprise of splashes that leap up as you stomp. Then, there's the tactile pleasure of squishing the oozing mud between your fingers, and letting drops of it drip, drip, drip and splash, splash, splash down into the puddle. The visual attraction of the puddle captures your child's attention too: The surface looks like a mirror, with flashes of color and moving images (the sun shining down on it after the rain, clouds passing overhead).

Of course, toddlers don't *think* about mud in this way, but they do *experience* it with all their senses. So next time there are some good mud puddles calling your child's name, grab her rubber boots and old play clothes (have a clean towel waiting at the back door), and go meet that puddle.

94 | PORTABLE SANDBOX

AGE:
2 years

CATEGORY:
Parent &
Child Play/
Outdoor

**NUMBER OF
CHILDREN:**
One

* SAFETY ALERT
Supervise your
child to make
sure he does not
eat the sand or
rub sand in
his eyes.

*This mini sandbox in a dishpan is just right for
first-time sandbox play for toddlers.*

Materials

▸ Small plastic tub with lid

▸ Clean play sand* (available at toy stores)

▸ Sandbox toys (sieve, sprinkling can, cups, rounded
sand tools)

Setup

Fill a plastic tub with clean, fine sand and take
it outdoors on the porch or patio.

Play

Fill containers with sand and then dump it
out! Rake the sand into patterns and put it
through a sieve. A sandbox is like a miniature
garden for a toddler. Add a bit of water to the
sprinkling can and let him experiment with
watering the sand and building with it.

ANIMAL PATROL

AGE:
2 years

CATEGORY:
Parent &
Child Play/
Outdoor

**NUMBER OF
CHILDREN:**
One

* SAFETY ALERT

Supervise your child when playing with sand. Sand play is best for toddlers who no longer put everything in their mouth and also for children who won't throw sand.

It's quite magical for a toddler to scoop up some sand with a strainer, give it a few gentle shakes, and discover an animal hiding inside the strainer.

Materials

▸ Small plastic tub with lid

▸ Clean play sand* (available at toy stores)

▸ Toddler-safe plastic animals

▸ Small kitchen strainer with handle

▸ Small bowl

Setup

Fill the tub with clean play sand and take it outdoors to the porch, patio, or stoop. Hide a handful of plastic animals (or figures) throughout. (Hide them close to the top, or bury them way down deep to increase the level of challenge according to your child's age, ability, and patience.)

Play

Show your child how to use the strainer to scoop sand; gently shake to unearth hiding animals. When your child finds an animal, she places it in the bowl and continues to look for more.

96 | PICNIC-PLATE FLOAT

AGE:
2 years

CATEGORY:
Parent &
Child Play/
Outdoor

**NUMBER OF
CHILDREN:**
One

* SAFETY ALERT
Constantly
supervise all
water play and
drain the pool
when the game
is over.

*Splashing, squishing, and squealing—oh my!
Take your toddler's shoes off for this wading-pool
Nerf-toss.*

Materials
▸ Wading pool*
▸ Plastic picnic plates with raised rims
▸ Nerf balls

Setup
Fill the wading pool with several inches of
water. Place the empty picnic plates in the
pool. (The more plates in the pool, the greater
the chance your toddler will land the ball on
the floating target!)

Play
Stand along the outside of the pool and toss
the Nerf ball onto one of the plates.

97 | TODDLER TAG

AGE:
2 years

CATEGORY:
Parent &
Child Play/
Outdoor

**NUMBER OF
CHILDREN:**
One

*Never underestimate the fun of
a good game of chase!*

Setup
You only need to modify this classic slightly for
your toddler. The format is simple: Ask your
child to run after you as you zigzag around the
yard or park.

Play

When she catches you, she touches you, and then you give chase and run after her. This toddler version is enhanced with silly movements, detours, and sound effects from you. If two adults are both willing to play, the three of you can take turns chasing one another around the lawn. The more the merrier, and it's good exercise for you too!

98 RUNNING AROUND TO LET OFF STEAM

PARENT TIP

"Some days my twenty-month-old son gets really frustrated playing with his giant LEGOs. When one of these moods strikes, I announce it's time for a game of chase outside and we move outdoors for a couple minutes of run-around play. It gives him a chance to let off a little steam, and the change of scenery helps to reset his mood. This is a quick-fix idea for frustration that almost always works with my toddler."

—Jonathan from Tennessee

BEACH DAY

Being near the ocean is a beautiful and powerful experience for people of every age, so imagine how exciting a toddler's first encounters with the vast expanse of salty water and grainy sand will be—it's like a giant bathtub or swimming pool right next to the world's biggest sandbox! The sights and sounds (squawking gulls and crashing waves) may be sensory overload for a two- to three-year-old, so wait until low tide to introduce him to the beach's many play opportunities.

99 BEACH PUDDLE

AGE:
2 years

CATEGORY:
Parent & Child Play/ Outdoor

NUMBER OF CHILDREN:
One

* SAFETY ALERT
This activity is best for older toddlers who won't put sand in their mouth or eyes. Always supervise all water play.

Splash in a shallow tidal pool and dig into the giant sandy beach!

Materials
▶ Plastic sand bucket and shovel
▶ Plastic sprinkling can
▶ Floating (bathtub) toys

Play*
Head to the beach shortly after high tide, with the plan to play in the shallow tidal pools created in the sand. (Or dig a shallow reservoir in the sand, several inches deep, and fill it with buckets of seawater to create a play-pond.) Plop yourselves into the tidal pool, begin filling the bucket and sprinkling can

with water, and float toys alongside the small pond. When this repetitious play wears thin, a little splashing and stomping in the water extends the excitement.

100 BIG WATER, LITTLE WATER

AGE:
2 years

CATEGORY:
Parent &
Child Play/
Outdoor

**NUMBER OF
CHILDREN:**
One

* SAFETY ALERT

This activity is best for older toddlers who won't put sand in their mouth or eyes. Always supervise all toddler water play.

A pond appears as you and your child scoop buckets of "big water" from the ocean.

Materials

▶ Plastic shovel

▶ Plastic cup and/or buckets

Play*

Dig a small pond (2 feet across and several inches deep) about 10 feet from the ocean or lake's edge. Give your child a plastic cup to dip into the water, and encourage her to carry it back to the pond to dump into the hole. Back and forth from the ocean (big water) to the pond (little water), filling and dumping. The pond takes shape if you fill a bucket and dump it each time your toddler empties her cup. Before long, your child will be splashing or stomping in the pond, creating a second round of play. Add a few tub toys and more fun unfolds.

LET IT SNOW!

Imagine for a minute the excitement your toddler experiences when introduced to snow for the very first time. He'll hear the crunch, crunch, crunch with each step he takes. His eyes will discover an entirely new outdoor world that is blanketed in white. And the feel of the snow is remarkable—it's cold, then wet, and then it begins to melt! All these discoveries are part of your child's play experience. A snowsuit, boots, and waterproof mittens keep the warmth in and the moisture out, allowing for an extended play day in the snow. Here are a few activities for outdoor, frosty fun together.

101 BUCKETS AND SHOVELS

AGE:
2 years

CATEGORY:
Parent &
Child Play/
Outdoor

**NUMBER OF
CHILDREN:**
One

Plastic sand buckets and small shovels are perfect for older toddlers who will enjoy filling the buckets with snow, dumping it out, and stamping the snow mounds with their feet.

Materials
▸ Plastic sand buckets of various sizes
▸ Small plastic shovels

Play
Bring along a few buckets and shovels while playing outdoors, and cue your child to shovel the snow into the bucket and to dump it out, creating mounds of snow. Both of you can stand atop the little hills to see what happens.

TRAIN TRACKS

AGE:
2 years

CATEGORY:
Parent &
Child Play/
Outdoor

**NUMBER OF
CHILDREN:**
One or more

If your child loves trains, or is simply mesmerized by the designs his feet make in the snow, he will thrill at this game.

Play

Shuffle your feet through the snow, making "train tracks" as you go. First, you are the locomotive in front, chug, chug, chugging along the tracks (add a few sound effects for this special winter express), with your child making his own tracks behind you. Then, switch places and let your child be the engine car, with you chug, chugging behind as the caboose.

One of the things a parent can do is really watch the baby. Pay attention to what the baby is touching or looking at or listening to, and take advantage of that. Let the baby be your partner and lead you into a natural everyday game."

—Sharon Landesman Ramey, PhD
research professor and research scholar at Virginia Tech
and coauthor of *Right from Birth*

103 | SNOWBALL DROP

AGE:
2 years

CATEGORY:
Parent &
Child Play/
Outdoor

**NUMBER OF
CHILDREN:**
One

Make a sport out of creating snowballs and watching with delight as they drop to the ground and disappear!

Materials

▸ Snow

Play

Pack a snowball and hold it in your hands. Let your toddler explore this fascinating "ball" by holding it in his own hands. Make another snowball, hold it high above your head, and drop it on a snowy patch of the lawn or on the sidewalk while your toddler looks on. Create more and more snowballs for your child to lift overhead and drop to the ground with delight. (What an amazing little ball that shatters or disappears when it is dropped, then more and more snowballs magically appear!)

104 SNOWBALL STOMP

Line up a row of ten snowballs on the ground. Use your boot to stomp one of the snowballs in the line and chances are your toddler will continue an enthusiastic game of Snowball Stomp with the other snowballs in the lineup.

SLEDDING

AGE:
2 years

CATEGORY:
Parent &
Child Play/
Outdoor

**NUMBER OF
CHILDREN:**
One

There is nothing more fun or memorable for a parent and child than a day of sledding in a winter wonderland. Pull your toddler around the park or your own backyard in a baby-safe sled.

Materials

▸ Baby-safe sled with rope pull

Play

Place your child in the sled and pull her around the park or yard. Although your toddler isn't ready for coasting downhill at top speed, she will still be absolutely delighted to have you pull her through the snow, safe and sound on flat ground.

3

PLAY WITH OTHERS

During your child's early years, development happens at such a quick pace; these changes affect the way your child plays. When one- to two-year-olds play around other toddlers, they are likely to play with their own toy in a solitary way. From time to time, these little playmates might glance at each other, but they will quickly move their attention back to their own toy. The early childhood development specialists call this "parallel play."

I call this type of play "side by side" because toddlers often warm up to each other by just coexisting in the same space. These favorite toys are a good bet for those times (it's best if each child has similar toys to play with and the freedom to direct his own play). You may need to get the play started by stacking blocks or rolling a ball down the slide or ramp. Be ready to step in to help resolve issues surrounding toys, turn-taking, and territory, which are the three sticky points when toddlers play together.

Here are some terrific toys that I recommend for side-by-side toddler play:

▸ Paper and crayons (*see page 51*)

▸ Dolls and doll accessories (*see page 58*)

▸ Cars and trucks (*see page 62*)

▸ Stuffed animals (*see page 63*)

▸ Blocks and giant LEGOs (*see page 65*)

▸ Ride-on toys, wagons, and shopping carts (*see page 66*)

▸ Dress-up props and toys (*see page 70*)

▸ Kitchen set and plastic foods (*see page 75*)

As toddlers get a bit older, they may continue to play side by side, but each child takes a bit more notice of what the other playmate is doing, perhaps imitating or incorporating those actions into their own play. Older toddlers may truly play together for short bursts of time. One child may be piling their blocks in a heap on the floor, and another might be pushing a cardboard box on the ground nearby. The block builder might drop a block or two into the box-driver's cart as they pass by. Seconds later, both resume their solitary play. If a friendly mood prevails, these fleeting moments of playing together might expand into honest-to-goodness cooperative play. On another day, these same little fellows might shun joint play for solitary play, drawing firm boundaries around their possessions. And so it goes when toddlers get together to play.

The best toys are the toys that have a lot of possibilities, as opposed to toys that do one thing."

—Alicia F. Lieberman, PhD
professor of psychiatry at the University of California, San Francisco,
director of the Childhood Trauma Research Project,
and author of *The Emotional Life of the Toddler*

INDOOR PLAY

Read through the selection of indoor ideas to see what activities might be just right for your child's next playdate. Keep in mind that because toddlers tend to play separately when they play together (side by side), it's best to have multiple props so there's plenty to go around—two chairs, two boxes, two stuffed bears! Conflicts will arise, but here are some strategies you can initiate to make playdates more harmonious:

▸ Accept the fact that your toddler doesn't like the idea of sharing (or giving up) his favorite toys when a playmate comes over. Move these special stuffed animals or toys to another room so that conflict doesn't arise.

▸ Expect a few disputes about possessions as toddlers play together. As you supervise, be ready to step in to redirect play and deal with hurt feelings.

▸ Include some larger toys and equipment (such as a toddler slide) that can't be grabbed by one child, so the children have some small opportunities to experience sharing and taking turns.

▸ As toddlers get older and show interest in truly playing together, offer toys that can be mixed together for short moments of cooperative play.

▸ Provide older toddlers with interesting props, playthings, and dress-up clothes for pretend play.

PRETEND PLAY

You'll see the very first hints of pretend play when your child imitates something he has seen others do. Perhaps your one-year-old tap-tap-taps his toy mallet on the wall, imitating you hanging a framed photo on the wall the night before. This imitative play offers a fascinating window into how many things your toddler notices. Eventually, these single actions morph into more elaborate pretend play where your child is acting out a sequence of events pieced together from recent experiences or created from his imagination. Your thirty-month-old daughter may pretend to pump gas into her ride-on truck, ride to the "store," and load up some "lumber" (wooden blocks). Much of this type of pretend play is created spontaneously when your child plays alone.

Some toddlers, particularly older toddlers, enjoy pretending with other children. Though pretending is often a spontaneous event, you can help set up pretend play for two or more toddlers. See pages 68–79 for suggested props and play ideas.

HOOPS

AGE:
1–2 years

CATEGORY:
Play with Others/
Indoor

**NUMBER OF
CHILDREN:**
Two

*A tossing game that is noncompetitive fun for two
or more toddlers. This game uses the simplest of
props and can be set up quickly.*

Materials

▸ 2 kitchen chairs (without any sharp edges or corners)

▸ Hula-Hoop

▸ Wide roll of painter's tape (or invisible tape)

▸ Balls (different colors, 1 for each child works best)
or a bucket of beanbags

Setup

Place two kitchen chairs in the middle of the
room, with the seats facing each other, spaced
about 22 to 25 inches apart. Rest the Hula-
Hoop across the seats of the chairs; it should
create a low hoop in which to toss the ball or
beanbags. Use the painter's tape to secure the
hoop to the chairs.

Play

Each child takes a turn tossing the balls
or beanbags into the hoop. Encourage the
children to stand as close to the hoop as
needed to launch the ball successfully.
Alternately, have two buckets of balls or
beanbags—one bucket for each child. In this
game, half the fun is launching all the balls
into the hoop. The other half is carrying the
bucket to the hoop to collect all the balls.

SOLID OBJECT DUMP AND FILL

AGE:
2 years

CATEGORY:
Play with Others/
Indoor

**NUMBER OF
CHILDREN:**
Two or more

*This free-form play may seem repetitive to you,
but for your toddler, it never gets old.*

Materials

▶ Empty container: plastic containers and bins; shoebox
with lid; oatmeal tub (cylindrical container); half-
gallon juice or milk cartons (top cut off); plastic
mix-and-pour bowls (with handle and pouring spout);
stainless steel mixing bowls and pans

▶ Objects for dumping: blocks; giant-size LEGOs; toy
animals and people; Wiffle golf balls; plastic food
container lids; large puzzle pieces; nesting cubes

Play

Your toddler may drag the empty container
from place to place, put objects inside (and then
drag it from place to place), tip the container
upside down, or fill the bucket with all the
objects and dump them out on the floor. There
are no rules, but your toddler may need a few
quick demonstrations of what can go inside, or
how items can be stacked in order to get started.

DUMP AND FILL

Adults may wonder why repetitive, seemingly futile dump-and-fill activities capture a toddler's attention, but there's actually a lot going on for one- to two-year-old children. On the simplest level, it's great fun to watch the action when you tip a tub of giant LEGOs on a wooden floor and they scatter about the room. Not to mention the resulting sound: an auditory exclamation point to the play! Dump-and-fill games are a good type of activity for two or more toddlers because each child can work independently with their own set of materials, while having the joy of watching another toddler do those same interesting motions. Young toddlers are typically attracted to the dumping, whereas older toddlers are often more interested in the filling action. Toddlers are also soaking up preliminary lessons about volume, gravity, cause and effect, and let's not forget the concepts of empty and full.

WATER DUMP AND FILL

AGE:
2 years

CATEGORY:
Play with Others/
Indoor

**NUMBER OF
CHILDREN:**
Two or more

* SAFETY ALERT
Supervise water
play carefully
and put only a
small amount
of water in the
plastic tub.

*Plop, drip, splash—the sounds from bathtime
transplanted to playtime.*

Materials

▶ Cotton area rug with nonslip backing or recycled
bathroom rug or vinyl tablecloth to place under the
play area

▶ Medium to large plastic tub or dishpan (or a portable
plastic infant bathtub or large stainless steel roasting
pan)

▶ Plastic measuring cups

▶ Kitchen funnels

▶ Plastic ice-cream scoop (one-piece, no small parts)

▶ Plastic cups, bowls

▶ Tub toys

▶ Small plastic colander, sieve, or strainer

▶ Squeeze bottles

▶ Waterwheel

Setup

Spread an area rug or vinyl tablecloth on the
floor to create a confined play area. Put 1 or 2
inches of water* in the plastic tub and place it
on top of the rug. Add toddler-safe tub toys and
cups for scooping and dumping inside the tub.

Play

Turn bathtime into playtime by using these
same water toys in the mini tub.

THE JOYS OF WATER PLAY

Toddlers are fascinated by the touch, taste, sound, sight, and smell of everything around them. It's easy to see why a small dishpan of water with a few floating toys and a couple of measuring cups offer great appeal and great fun for your toddler. Plunging little hands into the water alerts your child to its special cool, wet feel. This may prompt a few tastes to see what that wet stuff tastes like too. Tossing a rubber duck into the tub makes an impressive plop sound. How about dipping a measuring cup into the water, lifting it out, and pouring its contents back into the tub? All these actions and reactions create quite a thrilling playtime for your toddler.

109 I SPY GOOD SHARING

PARENT TIP

"A really fun way to reinforce positive sharing between toddlers is a game I call 'I Spy Good Sharing.' It does two things; it helps the very young kids realize that they can take charge and control their own behavior, which is a new concept for them. It also gives them a chance to notice what other people are doing and to step outside of that all-about-me phase that happens to the two- to four-year-olds. So, the next time your child or his playmate is doing a pretty good job sharing or taking a turn, remember to say, 'I Spy Good Sharing' as a quick and playful way to say, 'good job.'"

—Lauri from New Hampshire

BOX-CARS FOR TWO

AGE:
1–2 years

CATEGORY:
Play with Others/
Indoor

**NUMBER OF
CHILDREN:**
Two or more

*Boxes are among the very best toys for
freewheeling, open-ended play.*

Materials

▸ Shoeboxes or small cardboard boxes
(1 or more for each child)

▸ Blocks, toys, or stuffed animals

Play

Toddlers fill their shoeboxes with their
personal cargo, then push or pull their
box-car along the carpet or smooth floor.

111 COLORFUL BOX-CARS

For customized, colorful box-cars, cover the
outside of each box with colored construction
paper and invisible tape.

112 SHOEBOX GARAGES

See page 62 for turning shoeboxes into
garages and tunnels just right for plastic
cars and trucks.

113 CAMPOUT CAVE, ROCKET SHIP, OR AIRPLANE

For your older toddler, turn an appliance box
on its side and provide blankets or sleeping
bags, pots and pans, and gear for a pretend
campout adventure inside. Or stand the box
upright and let the toddlers step inside for a
pretend rocket ship or airplane journey. Let
the children use crayons or markers to add
color and designs to decorate the rocket ship.

ART PLAY

I absolutely love to watch two or three toddlers sitting side by side, engaged in simple art-play. One child picks up a chunky crayon and makes a few marks on paper. The other child watches intently. That second child picks up a crayon, and now it's the first child's turn to watch. Back and forth they go, creating, watching, and imitating one another. And just when things seem to settle in, with both artists scribbling away at the same time, one child reaches over and grabs a crayon from the other. This is the way that all budding artists and collaborators get their start.

114 GIANT TODDLER DRAWING FOR TWO

AGE:
1–2 years

CATEGORY:
Play with Others/
Indoor

**NUMBER OF
CHILDREN:**
Two or more

Turn your kitchen table into an enormous canvas, with lots of elbow room for each child to scribble. What a thrilling way to spend an afternoon!

Materials

▸ Roll of butcher paper or 4 to 5 paper grocery bags
▸ Invisible tape
▸ Assortment of chunky (preschool type) crayons
▸ Large unbreakable bowl

Setup

Completely cover your kitchen table with butcher paper. (If using paper bags, cut off the bottoms and make one lengthwise cut in each bag to create large flat pieces of paper. Completely cover the table with the brown paper.) Tape over all the seams so you end up with one giant coloring surface. Loosely tape the ends and sides to the table to hold it in place. Place a large bowl filled with crayons in the center of the table.

Play

Sit down with the children, grab a crayon, and begin drawing on any part of the paper; the children will follow suit and create their own scribbles and drawings. For added excitement (and as the paper gets covered with scribbles), tape a fresh piece of butcher paper in front of each artist. If the toddlers want their own picture to have and hold when scribble time is done, carefully remove the tape from the paper so that each child gets his very own drawing to take home.

CIRCLE PRINTS

AGE:
2 years

CATEGORY:
Play with Others/
Indoor

**NUMBER OF
CHILDREN:**
Two or more

★ SAFETY ALERT
Supervise
carefully and use
containers large
enough to not
pose a choking
hazard to infants
or toddlers.

*Toddlers like to watch shapes appear on the paper
and they like the repetition of this activity too.*

Materials

▶ Recycled tablecloth
(to devote to messy art
projects) or newspapers

▶ Construction paper

▶ Tape

▶ Nontoxic, washable
paint

▶ Plastic picnic plates

▶ Empty trial-size
(1.5 ounce) round
plastic lotion or
shampoo containers*

▶ Wet washcloths
(for cleanup)

Setup

Spread the tablecloth or newspaper over the
kitchen table for easy cleanup. Place a piece
of paper in front of each child. (For younger
toddlers, tape the paper to the tablecloth to keep
in place.) Pour 1 or 2 teaspoons of paint in each
plastic plate. Each child gets his own paint.

Play

Each child gets his own plastic bottle. He dips
the bottom of the container into the paint and
presses on the paper to create circle prints.
Most toddlers are happy with single-color
printmaking. If you want to expand this art-
play, provide two or three plates of paint with
containers for each child, designated to each
specific color so the paint colors don't get
mixed. Have wet washcloths on hand to move
in quickly when print time is over.

GIANT PRINTMAKING FOR TWO

AGE:
2 years

CATEGORY:
Play with Others/
Indoor

**NUMBER OF
CHILDREN:**
Two or more

* SAFETY ALERT

Best suited for
older toddlers
who do not
put things in
their mouths.
Supervise infants
or younger
toddlers carefully
and do not offer
them any small
stamps that could
pose a choking
hazard.

*It's impressive for a toddler to be given the green
light to scribble on such a giant surface.*

Materials

▸ Roll of butcher paper or 4 to 5 paper grocery bags

▸ Scissors (for adult use only)

▸ Invisible tape

▸ 2 large nontoxic ink pads

▸ Rubber printing stamps (with handle) in large circles,
  squares, other shapes, and an assortment of large
  letters* (available at teacher supply stores)

Setup

Completely cover your kitchen table with butcher
paper. (If using paper bags, cut off the bottoms
and make one lengthwise cut in each bag to
create large flat pieces of paper. Completely
cover the table with the paper.) Tape over all the
seams so you end up with one giant printmaking
surface. Loosely tape the ends and sides to the
table to hold it in place. Place one nontoxic ink
pad within easy reach of each child.

Play

Press one of the rubber stamps firmly into the
ink pad and press it on the paper as a quick
demo. Let the children create designs all over
the paper, while you provide supervision to
keep things safe and also settle minor disputes.

PLAY DOUGH

AGE:
1–2 years

CATEGORY:
Play with Others/
Indoor

**NUMBER OF
CHILDREN:**
Two or more

*I love the smell of play dough! It's also cheap,
colorful, and easy to share.*

Materials

▸ Vinyl tablecloth or recycled bedsheet or
tablecloth for easy cleanup

▸ Lots of play dough (play clay) in one color

▸ Plastic animals, figures, etc., to stand up in the
play dough

▸ Small margarine tubs

▸ Tiny rolling pin for each child

▸ Plastic cookie cutters, baby jar lids, or large LEGOs
for making imprints (or set of play dough tools)

Setup

Place the tablecloth or sheet on the table or
floor to designate the play area. Take the play
dough out of the containers and place it in the
center of the table or floor area.

Play

Give each child roughly the same (or similar)
clay toys (rolling pin, cookie cutter, etc.) to
work with. Children will enjoy sticking the
plastic figures in the dough and discovering
that they "magically" stand up. These toys also
make interesting impressions in the dough.
The margarine tubs make wonderful molds.
A toddler hand makes a fine, individual stamp
(and so does a foot!).

MUSICAL PLAY

Musical play for toddlers is more about experimenting with sounds and rhythm than it is about fine music making. But now that I've offered this disclaimer to prepare your ears and steady your nerves, let me also say that messing around with musical instruments (and banging on pots and pans) is a terrific way for your toddler to become acclimated to the idea that she has the power and potential to make "music."

118 MUSICAL CAKE PAN

AGE:
1 year

CATEGORY:
Play with Others/
Indoor

**NUMBER OF
CHILDREN:**
Two or more

Watching the ball go round and round and listening to the "music" it makes is fascinating and fun for toddlers.

Materials

▸ 1 or 2 plastic Wiffle golf balls

▸ Small, round metal cake pans (1 for each child) or cookie tins without lids (about 5 inches in diameter is the perfect size for small hands)

Setup

Put one plastic golf ball in the cake pan or cookie tin.

Play

Show the children how to hold both sides of the pan firmly. Have them move their hands and the pan from side to side (ever so slightly) to cause the ball to circle round and round the edge of the pan. The faster each child moves her hands from side to side, the faster the ball goes around and the more "music" she can make. It takes a little practice, but once she gets the hang of it, she'll be able to make a variety of sounds. (If her hands are holding on to the sides *and* the bottom of the pan, the sound is a bit softer or muffled. If she grabs only the sides, a clear, louder sound is created.) Once each child has perfected the movement needed to create the action and sounds, add a second Wiffle ball. Watch the two balls chase each other around the rim of the pan, and listen to a slightly deeper musical sound.

A child is more likely to be interested in singing if he sees an adult singing."

—John Feierabend, PhD
professor emeritus of music education
at the Hartt School at the University of Hartford,
and author of the First Steps in Music series

TODDLER BAND

AGE:
1–2 years

CATEGORY:
Play with Others/
Indoor

**NUMBER OF
CHILDREN:**
Two or more

★ SAFETY ALERT
These
instruments
are best for
toddlers older
than two.

Shake, rattle, 'n' roll! Toddler band practice always makes for a noisy good time. And who knows—maybe one day your grown-up musical genius will be able to say, "It all started in my parents' kitchen with a cowbell and a couple of baby rattles."

Materials

▸ Baby rattles
▸ Cong-Itas*
▸ Hand drums
▸ Large wooden train whistle*
▸ Maracas (toddler-style)

▸ Musical shakers*
▸ Rhythm sticks*
▸ Sand blocks*
▸ Tambourine*
▸ Triangle*
▸ Wooden clackers

A wonderful source for musical shakers and instruments for young children is Hearthsong (www.hearthsong.com).

Play

Sing a familiar toddler or preschool song (clap along to add a beat) or play favorite music, and give each musician an instrument to shake or tap. (See favorite songs, pages 92–95.) Most toddlers will need some adult direction for musical play with others, so be prepared to sing songs and demonstrate how to tap or shake each musical instrument to get things started. Embellish your child's musical play by adding simple hats or costumes and encouraging a march around the living room, parade style, for some spontaneous musical fun.

RATTLE 'ROUND THE ROOM

AGE:
2 years

CATEGORY:
Play with Others/
Indoor

**NUMBER OF
CHILDREN:**
Two or more

TIP

Animal shakers,
vegetable shakers,
or fruit shakers
are a few cleverly
shaped, toddler-
safe shakers for
children two years
and older—yes,
some of them are
decorated to look
like cucumbers,
peppers, eggplants,
carrots, apples,
oranges, lemons,
and bananas!

*Toddlers will shake, shake, shake all the way
around the room with this engaging game that
encourages kids to explore all the different
sounds they can make.*

Materials

▶ Assorted baby rattles and shakers
(2 for each child, 2 for parent demo)

Setup

Give each child her own toddler-safe musical
shakers (claim 1 or 2 shakers for yourself to
give a little demo).

Play

Since toddlers are marvelous imitators, show
them a few of your best music-making moves.
Encourage the children to shake their arms
or twirl in circles. To change things up, sing
some favorite songs for a round of toddler-
style dancing *and* music. Older toddlers (who
understand the concept of "stop and go")
may enjoy a version of Stop and Go Dancing
(page 197) in which they shake, shake, shake
while a song is sung or played, and hold the
shakers still and silent when the music stops.

121 TEDDY BEAR WALTZ

Let Teddy join in the fun by taping a small
rattle or musical shaker to his arm (using
invisible tape) so the children can make more
music together by dancing with their toys.

OUTDOOR PLAY

Outdoor play is active, providing fun and fitness for toddlers. Here are a few activities to keep two or more children playing happily side by side outdoors. Some of these games work best when each child has their own toys or props to play with (since toddlers are not yet masters at sharing). And, of course, your supervision is needed to help keep things on an even (and safe) keel as the children play together.

122 | TODDLER SOCCER

AGE:
2 years

CATEGORY:
Play with Others/
Outdoor

**NUMBER OF
CHILDREN:**
Two or more

There are no rules in Toddler Soccer. All you need to play are a couple of kids, a lawn, some playground balls, and a bit of stamina!

Materials

▸ Playground balls, with a different color for each child (trust me on this one!)

Setup

Distribute the balls and playfully demonstrate kicking a ball a little ways, running after it, and kicking it again, from one end of the lawn to the other.

Play

Some children will switch to rolling the ball or carrying the ball around the lawn, and that's fine too!

123 | SIDEWALK CHALK

AGE:
2 years

CATEGORY:
Play with Others/
Outdoor

**NUMBER OF
CHILDREN:**
Two or more

* SAFETY ALERT
Sidewalk chalk
is not safe for
toddlers who
still put things in
their mouths.

Toddlers are trying hard to figure out all the rules
of life. And then, out of the blue, you introduce
your child to sidewalk chalk and you say it's okay
to draw on the sidewalk! Life is full of rules and
happy surprises too.

Materials

▸ Sidewalk chalk*

▸ Small plastic containers
(margarine tub, Tupperware containers, etc.)

Setup

Place a few pieces of sidewalk chalk in each
container. Give each toddler her own tub of
chalk.

CLASSIC ACTIVITY

124 | LEAF BUCKETS

AGE:
1–2 years

CATEGORY:
Play with Others/
Outdoor

**NUMBER OF
CHILDREN:**
Two or more

Searching for fallen leaves in autumn is a
gratifying endeavor. Can you spot a yellow leaf?

Materials

▸ 2 small plastic buckets

▸ Leaves on the ground

Play

Toddlers love to carry their very own little
buckets for leaf gathering. When you get home,
start a leaf collection on your mantel so your
toddler can admire her treasures year-round.

WATER PAINTER

AGE:
1–2 years

CATEGORY:
Play with Others/
Outdoor

NUMBER OF CHILDREN:
Two or more

One of my son's favorite playtime activities when he was two was "painting" the sidewalk and porch steps with water. This can be fabulous summertime fun for toddlers.

Materials

▸ Small plastic buckets (1 for each child)

▸ Water*

▸ Paintbrushes with short, rounded handles and 2- to 3-inch bristles

▸ Paint tray and small paint rollers (alternative to buckets and brush)

▸ Bathing suits (optional)

Setup

Fill each bucket with about 2 inches of water. Prop up a paintbrush inside each bucket. (Or put 1 or 2 cups of water in a plastic paint tray and add a small paint roller to each tray.)

Play

Toddlers love to paint the deck, sidewalk, patio, railings, or deck furniture with water and paintbrush. In fact, they are very persistent painters, no matter that the designs evaporate in minutes from the sun overhead.

126 SHINING THE GRASS

AGE:
2 years

CATEGORY:
Play with Others/
Outdoor

**NUMBER OF
CHILDREN:**
Two

*Give the grass a squirt to make it shine and help
it grow! Toddlers love to "wash" outdoor furniture,
porches, and railings too.*

Materials

▸ Small plastic squirt bottles (1 for each child,
available at beauty supply shops)

▸ Water

Setup

Fill bottles with water.

Play

Use the water bottle to squirt and "shine"
the grass, as well as other outdoor items that
might need watering. You might find that
your toddler decides that she—or you—needs
watering too!

DON'T BITE BACK!

Often, one of the biggest toddler playtime problems is biting.
Address this issue by responding with a stern "no, you cannot do
that." Immediately remove the child from the situation to speak
with him alone about how biting hurts, and that it's a no-no. Until
he's ready to be brought back to the group, allow him to work on
a solo activity. Remind him that biting is not permitted, and then
reintroduce him to the group.

WADING POOL WATER PLAY

AGE:
1–2 years

CATEGORY:
Play with Others/
Outdoor

**NUMBER OF
CHILDREN:**
Two or more
(plus one adult
per child for
safety)

* SAFETY ALERT

Supervise your child while he is playing in the wading pool. If you have to leave, take your toddler out of the pool and keep him in your arms so he does not go near the water unattended. Also note that plastic tubs are slippery, so help your child in and out of the tub with care.

Splash around and grab at toys bobbing in the water. Use a sprinkling can to take a shower or wash a plastic doll. Find out what floats and what sinks! Warm weather water play is wet and riotous fun.

Materials

▶ Plastic tub, large dishpan, or wading pool*
▶ Toddler-safe tub toys
▶ Toy sprinkling can
▶ Plastic balls (for floating)

Setup

If using a tub or dishpan, pour in 4 to 6 inches of water to create a toddler-size wading pool.

"

A really important and positive rule children learn in playgroups is that fighting with each other, biting each other, pinching each other, does not mean the end of the relationship. One child can say 'I'm sorry' and can do something to appease the other, and things can again get better from there."

—Alicia F. Lieberman, PhD
professor of psychiatry at the University of California, San Francisco, director of the Childhood Trauma Research Project, and author of *The Emotional Life of the Toddler*

WASH THE BABY— OR THE CARS!

AGE:
1–2 years

CATEGORY:
Play with Others/
Outdoor

NUMBER OF CHILDREN:
Two or more

* SAFETY ALERT
Constantly
supervise all
water play
and drain the
dishpans when
you're finished.

Toddlers love to wash things on their own. They see you doing household chores all the time, and they want to do their part too! When two or more toddlers are splashing and scrubbing, "washing" something takes on a whole new dimension.

Materials

▸ Plastic cups

▸ Plastic dishpan (1 for each child)

▸ Washcloth or small sponge or plastic vegetable scrubber (1 for each child)

▸ Plastic dolls or plastic cars and trucks

Setup

Pour a couple of inches of water into each child's plastic dishpan. Add a plastic cup and sponge, washcloth, or vegetable scrubber to each tub. Be sure to give each child the same washing tools and cups (for rinsing and pouring) to avoid squabbles. To spice things up, add a floating toy to each dishpan to see what happens next. Scrubbing, pouring, and splashing will ensue.

LAUNDRY BASKETBALL

AGE:
1–2 years

CATEGORY:
Play with Others/
Outdoor

**NUMBER OF
CHILDREN:**
Two or more

A giant laundry basket is just the right prop for a happy game of toddler basketball. Though it's tempting to cheer your toddler on every time she makes a goal, I try to temper this instinct so as not to frustrate a toddler who's having difficulty with her slam dunk.

Materials

▶ Large plastic laundry basket, or multiple smaller baskets (1 for each child)

▶ Medium- to large-size plastic balls (or small playground balls) in varying colors (1 for each child)

Setup

Place the laundry basket on the lawn. Use your own ball to demonstrate how to toss the ball in the basket. Each child plays with her own colored ball.

> **"**
> You want to give children practice with solving their anger and frustration without you. Give them a start, but then move away and see if they can solve them on their own."
>
> **—Rebecca Kantor, EdD**
> dean of the School of Education and Human Development
> at the University of Colorado Denver

SCOOPER DUPER

AGE:
1–2 years

CATEGORY:
Play with Others/
Outdoor

**NUMBER OF
CHILDREN:**
Two

* SAFETY ALERT
Constantly
supervise all
water play and
drain the tubs
when you're
finished.

*Mix together two unlikely play props: plastic balls
and an ice-cream scooper and you have a flexible
game called Scooper Duper.*

Materials

▶ Ping-Pong balls

▶ 2 plastic gallon-size tubs
(ice cream tubs, for example)

▶ One-piece, molded plastic scooper
(without sharp edges or small parts)

Setup

Put the balls in one of the tubs. Put 1 or 2
inches of water in the other tub and place it
a few feet away on the lawn.

Play

The object is to scoop the balls from the tub one
at a time using the ice-cream scooper and drop
them (plop!) into the empty tub. Children one to
two years old will probably end up using their
hands. When the transfer has been completed,
the process can be reversed. (It's a bit more of a
challenge because of the water.)

4

PARTY
PLAY

Your toddler's first or second birthday is a marvelous occasion to celebrate—but it can also be a bit nerve-wracking. Short of hiring a fire engine or having a group of astronauts come by, how are you going to keep all those toddlers happily occupied? Look no further! Everything you need is in this section. But before you begin planning your child's party, here are a few key elements of the most successful toddler birthday parties to keep in mind:

▶ Low-key fun

▶ Toys for independent play

▶ Space to move about (indoors or outdoors)

▶ Group activities involving side-by-side play

▶ A few brief cooperative play ideas (ring-around-the-rosy, etc.) that children can join in or watch

▶ One adult to supervise every toddler

▶ Keep it short (sixty to ninety minutes at most)

You can design a splendid party for your child's first or second birthday by incorporating play ideas from the three main birthday activity categories you will find in this section— Parent & Me Party Activities, Play Stations, and Group Play. With a little mixing and matching of the play ideas in this section, you can create a terrific sixty- or ninety-minute party. You'll also see a sample First Birthday Party Itinerary and a Second Birthday Party Itinerary to give you suggestions of how to mix and match games and activities to create a

successful party. (But keep in mind that only you will know how to pace the party to suit the moods, interests, and abilities of the toddlers present, so by all means, let your own judgment determine how many toys and games to offer to keep your crowd happy.)

Parent & Me Party Activities are very short activities and crafts for parents and toddlers to enjoy together—decorating prebaked sugar cookies with frosting and sprinkles or making very simple birthday crowns from precut scalloped borders, for example.

Play Stations are play areas set up indoors or outdoors with appealing toddler toys and props (enough so that each child winds up with the same materials), including an assortment of balls, cardboard boxes, and plastic dishpans.

Group Play includes favorite activities for all the children to play together (side by side)—chasing bubbles on the lawn, pouring cups of water in a wading pool, using big paintbrushes or rollers to "paint" the sidewalk with water.

SAMPLE FIRST BIRTHDAY PARTY ITINERARY
(60 MINUTES)

ARRIVAL ACTIVITY (5+ minutes): Birthday Mural

PLAY STATIONS (15 minutes): Buckets of LEGOs or Blocks, Cars Go Zoom, Let's Play Ball

TIME FOR CAKE OR CUPCAKES (5 to 10 minutes)

PARENT & ME ACTIVITY (10 minutes): Super-Simple Toddler Crowns, Crumpled-Paper Toss, Sock Toss

Repeat Play Station Games Again

SAMPLE SECOND BIRTHDAY PARTY ITINERARY
(60 TO 90 MINUTES)

ARRIVAL ACTIVITY (5 to 10 minutes): Party Play Dough

PLAY STATIONS (20 minutes): Cars Go Zoom, Music Makers for All, Teddy Bear Picnic, B.Y.O. Scooter, Buckets of LEGOs or Blocks, Dress-Up

TIME FOR CAKE OR CUPCAKES (10 minutes)

PARENT & ME ACTIVITY (10 minutes): Treasure Boxes

GROUP PLAY (15 minutes): Paint Party, Walking the Plank, Stop and Go Dancing, Butterfly in the Garden

PARENT & ME PARTY ACTIVITIES

One great thing about toddler parties is that each child is accompanied by a parent or caregiver who will probably stay during the entire party. This means that all the children will be well supervised; it also provides opportunities for activities that toddlers and adults can do together. That way, each toddler gets individual attention and reassurance from someone special in their life, at the same time getting a taste of group play and excitement at the party. Here are some short, first-rate party play activities for parent or caregiver and child.

131 SUPER-SIMPLE TODDLER CROWNS

AGE:
1–2 years

CATEGORY:
Party Play/
Parent & Me

NUMBER OF CHILDREN:
Three or more

Use premade scalloped cardboard borders to make instant toddler crowns. The children will scribble and decorate and, just when their attention span is coming to an end, an instant crown appears on their heads.

Materials

▶ Butcher paper
▶ Pack of precut cardboard scalloped borders (available at teacher supply stores)
▶ Invisible tape (for adult use only)
▶ Crayons and nontoxic washable markers
▶ Color dot stickers (available at office supply stores)

TIP

The first time around, the toddlers probably won't understand what they are decorating. When they see one of the parents turning that masterpiece into a "hat" or crown that can actually be worn, the level of excitement will rise. For this reason, it's a good idea to have enough material for each child to make two crowns—one for a parent and one for herself!

Setup

Cover your entire kitchen table with the butcher paper and secure with tape to hold it down. Place a length of scalloped border on the table for each child, and use invisible tape to secure it to the butcher paper (making it easier for toddlers to color). Note that since the entire table will be scribbled on, the butcher paper becomes a lovely creative by-product from this craft.

Play

The children decorate their crowns using crayons, markers, and stickers. Grown-ups can help by peeling a corner of each sticker from the paper for easy toddler handling, or by holding the scalloped border in place while their child scribbles. When the decorating is done (or the child's good humor begins to disappear), the parents peel off the tape to remove the border from the table, cut the scalloped border to crown length, and tape the two ends together.

TREASURE BOXES

AGE:
1–2 years

CATEGORY:
Party Play/
Parent & Me

**NUMBER OF
CHILDREN:**
Three or more

This is a fun activity with a bonus—a take-home prize for each child. Why spend money on party favors when you can have the children handcraft their own?

Materials

▶ Child- or adult-size shoebox
(with lid, 1 for each child)

▶ Construction paper

▶ Color dot stickers
(available at office supply stores)

▶ Nontoxic glue sticks

▶ Crayons and nontoxic markers

▶ Scissors and invisible tape
(for adult use only)

Setup

Prior to the party, collect enough shoeboxes so that each child gets his own. (Visit your local shoe store to find recycled shoeboxes and repair with tape if needed.) Cut each piece of the construction paper into fourths. Fill each shoebox with one or two sheets of sticker dots, a glue stick, quarter sheets of construction paper in multiple colors, and three to four chunky crayons (make sure the contents of each shoebox are identical).

Play

Have the children scribble on or decorate their construction paper; when they're finished, the adults tape the pieces to the inside and outside

of the shoebox lid. Cut additional drawings to decorate the sides of the box. When the decorating is over, this becomes a terrific take-home party prize.

A PARTY PLAN FOR YOUR CHILD'S FIRST BIRTHDAY

Have simple expectations, try to make it fun, be flexible, and read your audience as the party gets under way. This is my very best advice about hosting a successful first birthday party for your child. Think of the party as a short, sixty- or ninety-minute playgroup with cake and a few photos thrown in for good measure, and you get the basic idea about what is achievable.

The unique challenge of planning a one-year-old's party revolves around the fact that some children won't yet be walking; others can walk but not run; and some are better at using their hands to maneuver and play than others. In short, you have quite a range of abilities, interests, and play styles to contend with. Here are a few first birthday party tips:

▹ Schedule the party early in the morning or after the afternoon naptime (so all children are in good humor).

▹ Keep the party short (sixty to ninety minutes is best).

▹ Rely on each parent or caregiver present to help supervise and play.

▹ Have a short birthday cake break during playtime, but realize that many of the children won't sit still for long.

HIDDEN STARS

AGE:
1–2 years

CATEGORY:
Party Play/
Parent & Me

**NUMBER OF
CHILDREN:**
Three or more

*The moon and stars are magical, faraway
wonders to a child. With a tiny bit of nudging
from a parent or a caregiver, each child can
find the hidden stars and pack them away
inside their very own party favor bags.*

Materials

▶ Brightly colored poster board (or purchase precut
cardboard stars at teacher supply stores)

▶ Pencil and scissors (for adult use only)

▶ Colorful gift bag with handles for each child
(available at party supply stores)

▶ Glitter glue, stickers, markers (optional)

Setup

Before the party, cut out one large, 6- to
8-inch cardboard star. Use it as a pattern to
trace more stars onto the poster board. Cut
out enough stars so that there are four to eight
for each child. Set aside one star per child.
Write each child's name on a star, decorating
with glitter glue, stickers, and markers, if time
permits. Deposit these personalized stars into
the gift bags and write each child's name on
the outside of the bag. Hide most of the other
stars all over the lawn (or throughout the
house), with at least part of each star in plain
sight. Keep a bag of extra stars that can be
quickly hidden while the hunt is wrapping up,
so that if some children have had less success
in their searches, you can nudge them and
their parents toward these remaining stars.

Play

Give each child their star-collecting bag. Each child's parent acts as the guide through the "finding" process. Since this game is not a competition—every child should find roughly the same number of stars—be prepared to give parents a few hints about where to look next or when their child is getting hot or cold.

134   PARTY PLAY DOUGH

AGE:
1–2 years

CATEGORY:
Party Play/
Parent & Me

**NUMBER OF
CHILDREN:**
Three or more

* SAFETY NOTE

This activity is
best suited to
children who no
longer put things
in their mouths.

The tactile quality of this play will keep the children absorbed and content for a while. It's an easy favorite for birthday parties.

Materials*

▸ Container of play dough (1 for each child)
▸ Tiny rolling pin (for play dough)
▸ Toddler-safe play dough tools
▸ Colored gift bag (with handles) for each child
▸ Large sheets of butcher paper and invisible tape

Setup

Prior to the party, put one can of play dough and a set of play dough tools in each gift bag. Write each child's name on the outside of their bag. Completely cover your table with butcher paper and secure with tape. (Or, cover a large area of your kitchen floor to create a giant play dough station.) Give each child a gift bag and a space at the table, and set them on the road to spontaneous play.

COOKIES WITH SPRINKLES

AGE:
2 years

CATEGORY:
Party Play/
Parent & Me

**NUMBER OF
CHILDREN:**
Three or more

NOTE

After about
30 minutes,
the frosting will
begin to harden
in the bowls;
right before the
party, thin it
with a bit of milk.

*This can be a bit messy, but it's yummy, gooey,
creative fun for toddlers!*

Materials

▸ Frosting:
  ▸ 2 cups confectioners' sugar
  ▸ 1 tablespoon milk, plus more as needed
  ▸ Food coloring (optional)
  ▸ Medium-size mixing bowl
▸ Small bowls (1 for each child)
▸ Small spoons (1 for each child)
▸ 1 or 2 jars of edible sprinkles
▸ Large sugar cookies (prebaked or store bought)
▸ Small ziplock bags
▸ Party bags with handles (1 for each child)

Setup

Make your own simple frosting a few minutes
before the party begins. Place 2 cups of
confectioners' sugar in your mixing bowl. Stir
in one tablespoon of milk at a time until you've
created a runny frosting about the consistency
of gravy. (Add a drop of food coloring if you
like.) Spread a tablecloth on the table and
scoop a small amount of frosting into each of
the small bowls. Place a bowl and a spoon at
each setting, and a jar of sprinkles nearby.

Play

Seat the children. Each child gets to decorate one or two large sugar cookies. Parents and toddlers work together to drizzle a spoonful of frosting on their cookie. Then the toddlers go to work shaking sprinkles on top. (Obviously, some of the children will sample their cookies or frosting as they create—it's all part of the game!) When cookie time is over, leave the cookies out on the table to dry. Have one adult helper come back later to put each cookie in a ziplock bag to go in each cookie artist's treat bag at the end of the party. One word of caution: Make sure to keep the family pet away from the cookie table, or you'll have some disappointed toddlers on your hands at the end of the party!

136 ANIMAL COOKIES STUCK IN THE MUD

Use brown food coloring (red and green food coloring mixed together) in the frosting, and have each child drizzle it over a giant sugar cookie. Before it sets, stick a few animal crackers in the frosting (the mud!). Sprinkles are the final touch in this elaborate cookie creation.

CRUMPLED-PAPER TOSS

AGE:
1–2 years

CATEGORY:
Party Play/
Parent & Me

**NUMBER OF
CHILDREN:**
Three or more

TIP

A little toddler-friendly, happy background music adds a nice touch while this activity is under way.

Parents make the paper balls and toddlers do the tossing. It's a super-simple game, but the children get a kick out of watching, listening to, and mimicking all the action going on—the sound of paper being scrunched, the sight of paper balls flying, and the busy bodies all around.

Materials

▸ 2 or 3 medium- to large-size cardboard boxes (or a few laundry baskets) placed around the room

▸ Recycled paper (100 sheets)

Setup

Place a cardboard box in the middle of the room. Parents and children should sit on the floor, scattered around the room. Give each parent a short stack of paper.

Play

Begin by having the parents scrunch the paper into balls (tightly squeezed so they're easier to handle). Parents demonstrate by either tossing the ball into the box or handing the ball to their child and helping them carry or drop it into the box. From this starting point, the game takes on a life of its own. The parents continue to make paper balls, and the children toss the balls into the box. Some children may want to scrunch up the balls on their own. Some may want to turn the box upside down or climb inside for a ride! (That's why it's a good idea to have a couple extra baskets or boxes on hand.)

PLAY STATIONS

I love the idea of having "play stations" at a toddler birthday party—designated play areas indoors or outdoors that have been set up (or stocked) with safe, enticing toys. My toddler play station motto is, *If you offer it, they will play.* If you place four balls in your backyard at a party with four toddlers, you can bet the children will begin playing with the balls.

The play that unfolds from these play stations will likely be a combination of solitary play (with each child tapping, swatting, rolling, and kicking the ball) and fleeting moments of joint play. Toddlers will follow the same model in their itineraries—they'll most likely move individually from station to station, rather than as a group. So children and parents may wind up scattered among several play stations, experimenting and playing.

138 B.Y.O. SCOOTER

AGE:
1–2 years

CATEGORY:
Party Play/
Play Stations

**NUMBER OF
CHILDREN:**
Three or more

* SAFETY ALERT
Provide constant
supervision to
ensure that the
children stay
clear of cars.

Materials
▸ Ride-on toys (1 for each child, provided by child's parents)
▸ Small buckets of water
▸ Washcloths or sponges (1 for each child)

Play*
Supervise the children while they play on their ride-on toys indoors, in a large playroom, or outdoors on the lawn or sidewalk. Give each child a small bucket of water and washcloth to create their very own "car wash" for their ride-on.

A PARTY PLAN FOR YOUR CHILD'S SECOND BIRTHDAY

I offer this mantra for a successful second birthday party: "Appealing toys and the opportunity to move about." Think of these little playmates as land rovers who move about to briefly investigate whatever strikes their fancy, stay a few minutes to play, and then move on again. This is why the play station idea is tailor-made for toddler birthday parties.

The second distinctive feature about two-year-old toddlers is that they love to walk, run, skip, hop, and dance. Physical movement of every sort is play for them. Build on this idea by including group games that encourage the children to romp around the room or lawn.

▸ Schedule the party for sixty to ninety minutes only, and select a time of day when everyone is well rested.

▸ Enlist the help of a few of the adults present when getting each game under way and corralling the children.

▸ Plan one arrival activity for toddlers and parents or caregivers to do together. (This helps the children adjust to the "group" in a secure way and is a good waiting activity as latecomers arrive.)

▸ Assemble toys and props to create a few play stations, and perhaps plan one or two short group games during the party. Plan to have birthday cake sometime in the middle or at the end of the party.

▸ Monitor the mood of the children and add high-energy play ideas to let off steam, or quiet-time activities to allow them to settle down as needed.

139 TEDDY BEAR PICNIC

AGE:
1–2 years

CATEGORY:
Party Play/
Play Stations

**NUMBER OF
CHILDREN:**
Three or more

Materials

▸ Assortment of stuffed animals
  (or B.Y.O.T.—Bring Your Own Teddy)

▸ Giant picnic blanket

▸ Miniature plastic cups, plates, and spoons

▸ Small containers (with lids) of safe finger foods
  for each child/teddy

▸ Shoeboxes and doll blankets (1 for each teddy)

Play

Lay the picnic blanket down and arrange
the place settings and snacks on top. The
shoeboxes can be used as chairs to prop up
the teddy bears for the picnic. Later, Teddy
can also curl up with his blanket and take
a nap inside his shoebox bed. If he wants to
go for a drive, Teddy can also ride around in
his fancy shoebox Cadillac. While children
are eating, you might read a quick teddy bear
story or recite a rhyme.

DRESS-UP BOX, AKA HATS GALORE

AGE:
1–2 years

CATEGORY:
Party Play/
Play Stations

NUMBER OF CHILDREN:
Three or more

Materials

▹ Large hatbox

▹ Children's and grown-ups' hats

▹ Wallets, purses, capes

▹ Sunglasses (with lenses removed)

▹ Large hand-held mirror for parent(s) to hold while the children check out their new looks

▹ Blanket (to spread on the ground)

▹ Teddy bears and stuffed animals

Play

Start out with the hats in the hatbox. This simple dress-up station will come to life when toddlers put hats on their own heads, on the teddy bears, or on their parents. And when they behold the magical transformations in the mirror, more glee ensues.

TWIRLING SCARVES AND STREAMERS

Older toddlers might enjoy waving scarves or streamers around to music. Provide each child with a long silk scarf or crepe-paper streamer and show them how to wave their arms up and down and side to side to make the streamer dance.

141 LET'S PLAY BALL

AGE:
1–2 years

CATEGORY:
Party Play/
Play Stations

**NUMBER OF
CHILDREN:**
Three or more

Materials

▶ Soft, medium-size balls for indoor play;
playground balls for outdoors (1 for each child)

▶ Slide

▶ Cardboard boxes, plastic baskets, or crates

Play

Toddlers will tap, roll, kick, chase, and toss
the ball (alone or with grown-ups or other
toddlers), send it down a slide, or drop it in
a box.

142 MUSIC MAKERS FOR ALL

AGE:
1–2 years

CATEGORY:
Party Play/
Play Stations

**NUMBER OF
CHILDREN:**
Three or more

Materials

▶ Cowbells, rattles, shakers (see page 160 for
finding toddler and preschool music makers)

▶ Crowns or party hats (1 for each child)

▶ Capes (1 for each child)

▶ Streamers

Play

Toddlers experiment with their music makers;
add props so older toddlers can create a musical
parade.

WATER PLAY

AGE:
1–2 years

CATEGORY:
Party Play/
Play Stations

**NUMBER OF
CHILDREN:**
Three or more

* SAFETY ALERT
Always
supervise
toddler
water play.

Materials

▶ Plastic dishpan or large disposable roasting pan (1 for each child)

▶ Plastic cups and containers

▶ Tub toys (rubber duck, fish, or boat—1 for each child)

▶ Towels (for spills or drying wet children)

Play

Place each of the small plastic pans on the deck or patio or lawn (with beach towels or washable blankets underneath) and fill with a few inches of water.* Provide plastic cups and tub toys, and each toddler will invent his own fun.

The best advice is to keep the birthday plans simple, especially when children are young. An elaborate or expensive birthday party is not going to be more fun or go more smoothly than just a simple party at home."

—Shelley Butler
coauthor of *The Field Guide to Parenting*

CARS GO ZOOM

AGE:
1–2 years

CATEGORY:
Party Play/
Play Stations

NUMBER OF
CHILDREN:
Three or more

NOTE
1 sheet makes
2 ramps; buy
enough so each
child has a ramp.

Materials

▶ Sheets of 20-by-30-inch foam board
(poster board with foam backing)

▶ Yardstick

▶ Scissors or utility knife to cut foam board
(for adult use only)

▶ Invisible tape

▶ Small, toddler-safe toy car (1 for each child,
or B.Y.O.C.—Bring Your Own Car)

Setup

Before the party begins, cut each piece of foam
board in half lengthwise to create individual
10-by-30-inch ramps for each of the attendees.
Use the yardstick as a guide to score and cut
one side; then flip it over, fold it in half, and
cut along the crease to create two ramps. (It's
a good idea to create one or two extra ramps,
for a quick exchange, in case one of the ramps
gets bent.) Prop the foam board ramps against
a sofa or chair at an angle. These ramps will
stay in place when positioned on carpet; if
you're placing them on a hard floor, use strips
of invisible tape to hold them in place.

Play

Give each child one or more toddler-safe cars
and a quick demo showing them how to zoom
the car down the ramp. These ramps and cars
are marvelous take-home party prizes too.

145 | BUCKETS OF LEGOS

AGE:
1–2 years

CATEGORY:
Party Play/
Play Stations

**NUMBER OF
CHILDREN:**
Three or more

Materials

▶ Giant LEGOs or wooden blocks
▶ Small buckets with handles or shoeboxes
(1 for each child)

Play

Place LEGOs or blocks in the buckets or boxes. Hauling, dumping, tower building, and tower crashing will ensue. Allow for enough elbow room so that each child can build and knock down his blocks. At the end of the party, the blocks stay at your house, but send the box or bucket home with the children with small party favors inside.

> The more you can involve others in the effort to lead a simpler, saner, slower life, the better. It's as easy as, 'Come on over Saturday and bring a dish, and we'll all play in the backyard.' What matters is that you get together and enjoy each other's company. People will thank you."
>
> **—Edward Hallowell, MD**
> psychiatrist and author of
> *Driven to Distraction* and *CrazyBusy*

GROUP PLAY

When things are going well, it's so interesting to sit back and watch a group of toddlers play. They have a funny little group dynamic. Some children focus exclusively on their own toys and scarcely notice other playmates. Others relish short moments of playing with other children and imitating their hilarious play ideas.

In this section, you will find noncompetitive, open-ended group play activities that allow lots of room for individual tastes. There's a little something for everyone. These "games" really don't have rules, and they don't require everyone's participation. Simply think of these activities as "play opportunities," and keep an open mind about the various ways the play might evolve.

146 | BUBBLE-CLAPPER

AGE:
1–2 years

CATEGORY:
Party Play/
Group Play

**NUMBER OF
CHILDREN:**
Three or more

I'll bet there are at least one or two bubble-clappers in the crowd just waiting to chase those elusive bubbles around the lawn.

Materials
▶ Small jar of bubbles and bubble wand (for each grown-up)

Play
You use the wand and bubble solution to blow bubbles, and your toddler tries to catch the bubbles (using her hands) or she claps them between two hands to make them pop. This is a simple but captivating activity to play with toddlers. (Older toddlers will enjoy playing outdoors and chasing the bubbles.)

WALKING THE PLANK

AGE:
2 years

CATEGORY:
Party Play/
Group Play

**NUMBER OF
CHILDREN:**
Two or more

This game combines the joys of physical and pretend play. Maybe there's a giant mud puddle surrounding the plank (excellent for stomping and jumping!), and maybe that puddle is filled with turtles and frogs and who knows what else. . . .

Materials

▸ Wooden board (no nails or jagged edges)

▸ 2 or 3 old beach towels

Setup

In a safe, flat, grassy area, place the board on the ground. (For older toddlers with better balance, roll or fold the beach towels and place them underneath the board at intervals to raise the plank by a couple of inches.)

Play

Ask (or show) the children to "walk the plank" without falling off the edge and see what happens!

148 BUTTERFLY IN THE GARDEN

AGE:
2 years

CATEGORY:
Party Play/
Group Play

**NUMBER OF
CHILDREN:**
Three or more

*Easy butterfly cocoons, arms, and legs are all you
need for this simple and active game.*

Materials

- Medium- to large-size
  cardboard boxes (boxes
  12-by-18 inches are
  ideal, 1 for each child)

- Beach towels or blankets
  (1 for each child)

- Scissors (for adult
  use only)

Setup

Remove box flaps and trim the sides of the
boxes down to about 6 inches to create a little
butterfly bed that each butterfly can easily
climb into. Place a crumpled beach towel
inside each box to create a cozy bed. Or, if you
are playing indoors (or very young toddlers
are playing), create little beds on the floor
using only the blankets (so that the butterflies
don't have to climb into their beds).

Play

When the butterfly fairy says, "Fly, little
butterflies, fly," the toddlers run and flap
their "wings" (arms); when the fairy says,
"Butterflies go to sleep," the toddlers pretend
to go to sleep in their butterfly beds. Start the
game by giving little demos to show how to
fly like a butterfly (run around flapping your
arms) and how a butterfly goes to sleep. After
the children get the idea and know where their
own butterfly beds are, call out, "Fly, little
butterflies, fly!" and let the flapping begin.

BIRTHDAY MURAL

AGE:
2 years

CATEGORY:
Party Play/
Group Play

**NUMBER OF
CHILDREN:**
Three or more

Your child doesn't need to wait until college to join an artistic cooperative; start her off early with this fun and easy group drawing project. If you've got good adult helpers in the mix, drawing is a great way to keep the toddlers focused and out of the way while you set up the cake in the kitchen.

Materials

- ▶ Roll of butcher paper
- ▶ Invisible tape
- ▶ Large, unbreakable bowl
- ▶ Big assortment of chunky crayons

Setup

Completely cover your kitchen (or picnic) table with butcher paper. Tape all the seams together to create one giant coloring surface and loosely tape the ends and sides to the table to hold it in place. Place the large bowl in the middle of the table and fill it with an assortment of crayons. (If you prefer, the activity can also take place on the floor.) Start off the mural by drawing a birthday cake with one or two candles in the center of the paper.

Play

Scribble-fest! If attention starts to wander and the party is in need of some direction, have the parents trace their child's hand on the mural and write their child's name near the hand. After the party, this will make a nice keepsake for you and your birthday boy or girl.

150 | # RING-AROUND-THE-ROSY

AGE:
2 years

CATEGORY:
Party Play/
Group Play

**NUMBER OF
CHILDREN:**
Three or more
(plus one adult
helper)

Songs are a great way to bring people together (big and small). And in the sometimes overwhelming chaos of a birthday party setting, the children will find comfort in a familiar song.

Play

The adult and all the children stand around in a circle holding hands. As you sing the song (below), everyone begins to move the circle in a clockwise or counterclockwise direction. When you sing the last line of the song, ("We all fall down"), you all suddenly sit down on the floor. This is always a very giggly moment for the toddlers, who'll insist on playing again and again.

Ring around the rosy,

A pocket full of posies,

Ashes, ashes,

We all fall down!

PAINT PARTY

AGE:
2 years

CATEGORY:
Party Play/
Group Play

**NUMBER OF
CHILDREN:**
Three or more

* **SAFETY ALERT**
Supervise all
water play
constantly and
dump out the
water once
you're through
playing. Stay in
a safe area, away
from cars and
traffic.

*Don't panic—the "paint" in this game is actually
water! Paint Party is always a crowd-pleaser, and
cleanup is over in the blink of an eye.*

Materials

▶ Plastic buckets or dishpans

▶ Chunky, round-handled exterior paintbrushes
(1 for each child)

▶ Small paint rollers (1 for each child)

Setup

This game takes place on a concrete patio or
sidewalk. Fill the buckets or dishpans with
a few inches of water.* Place all the brushes
and rollers on the ground near the buckets.
Show the toddlers how to pick up a brush and
begin "painting" the patio surface or sidewalk;
have another grown-up demonstrate how to
use the roller.

Play

Put your birthday party to work painting and
rolling away.

STOP AND GO DANCING

AGE:
2 years

CATEGORY:
Party Play/
Group Play

NUMBER OF CHILDREN:
Two or more
(plus an adult
helping with
music)

Start the music and everyone dances. Stop the music and all the dancers sit down. A great way to get a dose of dancing and an element of Simon Says into your party.

Materials

▸ Music player and music

Play

When you start the music, all the little dancers should begin to wiggle, shake, and twirl. (To get everyone going, you'll need to be a dancer too.) About 20 seconds later, stop the music and call out, "All the dancers sit down!" Repeat. As the children get the idea, stop and start the music at shorter intervals to create a stronger element of surprise.

153 MUSICAL RUNAROUND

Create a similar game with music that might include waving hands, clapping, jumping, or hopping to the music. All the action stops as soon as the music stops.

154 SOCK TOSS

AGE:
1–2 years

CATEGORY:
Party Play/
Group Play

**NUMBER OF
CHILDREN:**
Two or more

That large heap of socks in your living room isn't a load of unfinished laundry—it's the main ingredient in this active, risk-free game of indoor tossing and dumping. And if your socks don't match, no one will be the wiser!

Materials

▸ Lots and lots of socks
▸ Large cardboard box or laundry basket
▸ Large book
▸ Shoeboxes (1 for each child)

Setup

Create several dozen sock-balls, rolling each sock or pair of socks into a tight ball. Position the cardboard box on the floor, propped up against the sofa. (Put a large book under the back edge of the box so it is propped at an angle for easier tossing.) Put all the sock-balls in a large heap a few feet away from the box.

Play

The children grab balls and toss them into the basket. When all the socks have been tossed, they dump the box over on its side and toss all the balls back into a heap in the center of the room. (You might also want to set up a shoebox for each child, providing an alternate tossing target so some toddlers can play solo style; the shoeboxes are also terrific for spontaneous use as "cars" to be pushed around the room.)

HOOP-DEE-DO

AGE:
1–2 years

CATEGORY:
Party Play/
Group Play

NUMBER OF CHILDREN:
Two or more

A Hula-Hoop is a perfect target for a game of beanbag toss. And if you've got any hula experience under your belt, you might want to cap the afternoon with a demonstration of your prowess.

Materials

▸ Large Hula-Hoop
▸ Beanbags
▸ Small plastic buckets or bowls (1 for each child)
▸ Whistle on a string or a bell (for adult use only)

Setup

Place the Hula-Hoop on the ground on a safe grassy playing area. Put beanbags in each bucket or bowl so that every child has his own bags to toss.

Play

The toddlers stand around the outside of the hoop, a few feet away, and toss the beanbags into the center. Blow the whistle as a signal for all the children to go inside the circle and retrieve their beanbags.

FAMILY GAME NIGHT

One first-rate way to vote *yes* for family playtime is to create a Family Game Night that both parents and children can count on. Put it on your calendar, once a month or once a week, and make a commitment to this family tradition. (Yes, even during the teen years.) Of course, what you do together will change as the children move through each stage of their development, but the main ingredients remain the same—fun, play, and time together!

WHAT GOES ON AT FAMILY GAME NIGHT?

Here are a few words of wisdom to make your Family Game Night successful and exciting. Start with some easy foods like pizza or sandwiches eaten picnic style on a blanket on the floor, or decide to have breakfast for dinner. Set aside two hours for the event, and select a variety of games. (Nearly everyone will get bored with ninety minutes of playing one board game.) You may find it best to play two short, silly games that require a bit of moving around, followed by a guessing game or two. Create your personalized Family Game Night to suit your family's style, interests, ages, and individual personalities. Toddlers love to be included in the fun and excitement of family games. (Babies will be fascinated watching and listening to all the sounds and action too.) So, without further ado, here are the best games in this book for family playtime.

GAMES THAT REQUIRE MOVING ABOUT INDOORS

To get everyone engaged and their energy up, a few active games are just the thing. Pick a few to try, taking into consideration the age range of the children playing, and then move on to a game around the kitchen table.

▸ Color Dot Hide-and-Seek, page 106

▸ Follow the Leader, page 130

▸ Hidden Stars, page 178

▸ Musical Cake Pan, page 158

▸ Sock Toss, page 198

▸ Stop and Go Dancing, page 197

▸ Toddler Basketball, page 126

GAMES PLAYED AT THE KITCHEN TABLE

The kitchen table is a bustling center of family activity, and why should it stop after the last dish is cleared after dinner? Save the dishes for later—it's time to play!

▸ Paint Dabber, page 118

▸ Ringer-Ball, page 125

▸ Roller-Painting, page 120

▸ Scribble Lunch Bags, page 110

▸ Scribble Bookmarks, page 112

▸ Torn Paper Collage, page 114

GAMES FOR OUTDOORS

When the weather outside is warm (and far from frightful), here are a few suggestions for outside play that the whole family can get in on.

▸ Hoop-Dee-Doo, page 199

▸ Bubble-Clapper, page 191

▸ Paint Party, page 196

▸ Walking the Plank, page 192

THE WELL-STOCKED TODDLER TOY CUPBOARD

FOR FREESTYLE PLAY

- Balls (playground balls, Wiffle balls, tennis balls, Ping-Pong balls)
- Barn and farm set (includes animals)
- Beanbags
- Blocks (wooden, plastic, giant cardboard)
- Books for read-aloud (see pages 96–98 for a list of favorite toddler books)
- Bowls (unbreakable)
- Bubbles (adult supervision)
- Cars and trucks
- Doll stroller
- Dolls and doll accessories (baby bottle, crib, blankets)
- Dress-up hats, purses, wallets, backpacks

- Giant bead-maze (the type found in many doctors' office waiting rooms)
- Giant LEGOs
- Giant (plastic) popping beads
- Hula-Hoops
- Jack-in-the-box
- Kitchen set and plastic foods
- Miniature wagon
- Nesting cubes and blocks
- Peg-board with giant pegs
- Plastic animals
- Plastic lawn mower
- Plastic slide
- Plastic spinning top
- Plastic or wooden tool set (toddler-safe)
- Play dough and tools

- Play grocery cart and groceries (empty yogurt containers, pudding boxes, rice boxes, etc.)
- Playing cards
- Pop-up activity boxes
- Pots, pans, and cooking toys
- Pounding bench with plastic or wooden hammer
- Pretend money
- Pretend picnic set (plastic or wooden)
- Pull-toys
- Puppets
- Push toys
- Puzzles (lift-out style)
- Ride-on toys (without pedals, propelled by scooting feet)

- Sandbox and clean sand
- Sandbox toys
- Shape-sorting cube
- Sprinkling can
- Stacking rings
- Stacking wooden clown
- Stuffed animals

- Swings (toddler-safe)
- Tea set (unbreakable)
- Toddler-size cleanup toys: little broom, dustpan
- Toddler tool set (chunky plastic hammer, saw)
- Toy camera

- Toy phone
- Tub toys
- Wading pool (adult supervision)
- Waterwheel (plastic tub toy)
- Wooden or plastic people and animals
- Wooden or plastic toy train
- Wooden train

HOUSEHOLD ITEMS

- Bedsheets and tablecloths
- Cardboard boxes, shoeboxes, and hat boxes
- Cardboard tubes
- Cloth napkins
- Cookie sheets
- Dress-up clothes
- Egg cartons (cardboard)
- Envelopes (new or junk mail)
- Fishnet (tiny, used for fish tanks)
- Funnel
- Laundry basket (plastic)
- Measuring cups and spoons

- Metal roasting pan
- Muffin tins
- Notepad
- Office supplies (toddler-safe)
- Paint rollers and sponges
- Paper and/or cloth grocery bags
- Pillowcases
- Plastic and/or cardboard containers (margarine tubs, Tupperware, spice jars, tennis ball tubes, cups, yogurt cartons, milk jugs, bottles, diaper wipe boxes, etc.)

- Plastic colander or kitchen strainer (no small parts)
- Plastic cookie cutters
- Plastic or paper disposable plates
- Plastic ice-cream scoop
- Plastic lids
- Plastic wastebasket
- Pots, pans, safe kitchen utensils, measuring cups, bowls
- Salt and pepper shakers (unbreakable and empty)
- Scarves

IS IT A GOOD TODDLER TOY?

There are loads of colorful and attractive toddler toys on the market. You've probably discovered that some of these toys have true staying power and others are more ho-hum. Of course you'll need to select toys that seem to captivate your child's individual likes and toddler passions, but here are some general guidelines to keep in the back of your mind. A toddler toy should be:

1. SAFE Does it meet the following guidelines?:

▶ Made from durable, nontoxic materials.

▶ No small parts that can come loose (and create a choking hazard), including balloons.

▶ No sharp edges or corners.

▶ No long, loose strings or cords that could cause a strangulation hazard.

2. AGE APPROPRIATE Toys should cater to your child's physical and mental capabilities. Keep in mind that the toy manufacturer's recommended age for play is just a suggestion and might not tell the whole story concerning your child's matchup with this toy. Also, toddlers do become frustrated rather easily, so be sure to avoid toys that are far too difficult to manipulate or handle. (A toy that is a little challenging is good, but too much challenge can be overwhelming for your child.)

3. INTERESTING OR FASCINATING Toddlers love to make things happen—action is the name of the game. Particularly look for toys that your child can use or manipulate in multiple ways. A medium-size ball, for example: Your child can roll it and chase it across the floor, push it off the couch and watch it bounce from place to place, put it in a basket and dump it out, swat at it, and discover many other spontaneous ways to play.

- Shovels (plastic and toddler-safe)
- Socks
- Towels (bath, hand, dish, beach, washcloth)
- T-shirts (adult-size)
- Water bottles and squirt bottles
- Whistle
- Wooden clothespins

FOR ARTS AND CRAFTS

- Cardboard or foam board
- Cardboard scalloped-edge border (pre-cut)
- Chalkboard and chalk*
- Child-size rolling pin
- Colored gift bags
- Crayons*
- Flour and/or cornmeal
- Flour tortillas
- Food coloring (adult use)
- Glue (sticks, liquid, glitter), all nontoxic
- Library pockets
- Nontoxic finger paint*
- Nontoxic markers*
- Paintbrushes with short handles*
- Paper (butcher, notebook, copy, construction, newsprint)
- Plastic nonspill paint pots*
- Plastic pencil pouch
- Poster board
- Ruler
- Safety scissors*
- Scraps of ribbon and fabric
- Streamers
- Three-ring binder
- Tissue paper or wrapping paper
- Washable paints (nontoxic)
- Waxed paper*
- Wooden board (no nails or jagged edges)
- Wooden paint sticks or giant craft sticks*

Note: An asterisk indicates that the toy is suitable only for older toddlers, typically ages two and a half to three, who have stopped putting everything in their mouths.

FOR MUSIC

- Cong-Itas*
- Hand drums
- Jingle bells*
- Maracas (toddler style)

- Pots and pans with safe spoons for tapping
- Rattles
- Rhythm sticks*
- Sand blocks*

- Shakers
- Tambourine*
- Triangle*
- Wooden clackers
- Wooden train whistle

MUSICAL PLAY PROPS

The only electronic gear mentioned in this book, these props provide music for many classic movement games.

- Music and music player

Note: An asterisk indicates that the toy is suitable only for older toddlers, typically ages two and a half to three, who have stopped putting everything in their mouths.

PARENT PLANNER

OUR FAMILY FAVORITES

- Game: _____ PAGE: _____
- Game: _____ PAGE: _____
- Game: _____ PAGE: _____
- Game: _____ PAGE: _____
- Game: _____ PAGE: _____
- Game: _____ PAGE: _____
- Game: _____ PAGE: _____
- Game: _____ PAGE: _____

GAMES WE INVENTED

▶ Game: _____

▶ Materials: _____

▶ Play: _____

_____

_____

▶ Variations: _____

_____

_____

▶ Game: _____

▶ Materials: _____

▶ Play: _____

_____

_____

▶ Variations: _____

_____

_____

▶ Game: _____

▶ Materials: _____

▶ Play: _____

_____

_____

▶ Variations: _____

_____

_____

UNFORGETTABLE MOMENTS IN PLAY

▶ Child: _____ DATE: _____

▶ Game: _____

▶ What happened: _____

_____

_____

_____

_____

_____

▶ Child: _____ DATE: _____

▶ Game: _____

▶ What happened: _____

_____

_____

_____

_____

_____

▶ Child: _____ DATE: _____

▶ Game: _____

▶ What happened: _____

_____

_____

_____

_____

_____

INDEX

ACKNOWLEDGMENTS

This book is built upon the play experiences of real children who have engaged in all sorts of creative, active play. Let me begin by thanking my own children, Cassidy, Olivia, and Peter, for being such enthusiastic unplugged players during every stage of their childhood. Their exuberant, clever play ideas are woven into each section of this book.

I am deeply indebted to the fabulous game brainstormer and play reviewer (and extraordinary mom) Kiki Walker. Her marvelous can-do attitude made the research phase of this book a delightful experience.

Thank you also to the following children and parents who provided play ideas and tested games: Lakeshia Alexander; Carol Brown; Tom Daldin; John, Molli, Samantha, and Patricia Dowd; Jonnie, Bud, Andrew, Christian, Joanna, and Mary Grace Furmanchik; Anne, Ed, Claire, and Sam Gutshall; Ann Jenkins; Virginia McCann; Fulton and Ren Millis; Rob, Susan, Teddy, Julia, and Daniel Monyak; Christina, Chris, Jack, Kate, and Lucy Oxford; Liz and Bob Sauntry; Duncan, Lisa, Will, and Catherine Sherer; Els Sincebaugh; Breonna Tiller; Jacob Ufkes; Doug, Jack, George, Harry, and Lucy Walker; and Debbie Willis. Olivia Conner's creative thinking skills and artistic talents helped shape many of the arts and crafts projects in the book.

In my professional life, I have had the great pleasure of interviewing hundreds of wise and compassionate child development specialists about play, friendships, growing, and learning in my twenty-one years as host of *The Parent's Journal* public radio show. I offer a special thanks to these childhood experts, who have generously shared their insight, words of wisdom, and interview quotes in this book. (Julia Vanderelst stayed busy typing hundreds of hours of program transcripts from *The Parent's Journal* to capture these quotes.) Also, I could not have written this book without the dedication of my radio coworkers: Ellen Pruitt, Bruce Roberts, and Madeleine Thomas.

My first-rate agent (and terrific human being), Jim Levine, found just the right publisher for my book. Nina Graybill wears two hats marvelously well—both talented writer and outstanding attorney—and her advice and suggestions are much appreciated.

The exceptional team at Workman has made the publishing of this book a wonderful, collaborative experience. In the beginning, Peter Workman gave his enthusiastic "yes" to the importance of unplugged play. Megan Nicolay and Rachael Mt. Pleasant have been outstanding editors and delights to work with, providing creative ideas, careful editing, and great attention to detail. Suzie Bolotin nurtured this book from start to finish, offering a brilliant combination of encouragement, review, and fine editing along the way. The splendid art, illustrations, typesetting, and design provided by Bart Aalbers, Barbara Peragine, and Rae Ann Spitzenberger capture the essence of children at play and provide an easy-to-navigate format. Others at Workman I especially wish to thank are Angie Chen, Doug Wolff, Abigail Sokolsky, and Claire Gross. It has been a great pleasure to work with each and every one of you.

ABOUT THE AUTHOR

Bobbi Conner was the creator, producer, and host of the nationally syndicated public radio program *The Parent's Journal* for more than twenty years. She is the author of six books for parents and children, including *Everyday Opportunities for Extraordinary Parenting*, *The Book of Birthday Letters*, and *The Giant Book of Creativity for Kids*. She lives in Charleston, South Carolina.